OCS Study
MMS 2002-064

Coastal Marine Institute

Lagrangian Study of Circulation, Transport, and Vertical Exchange in the Gulf of Mexico

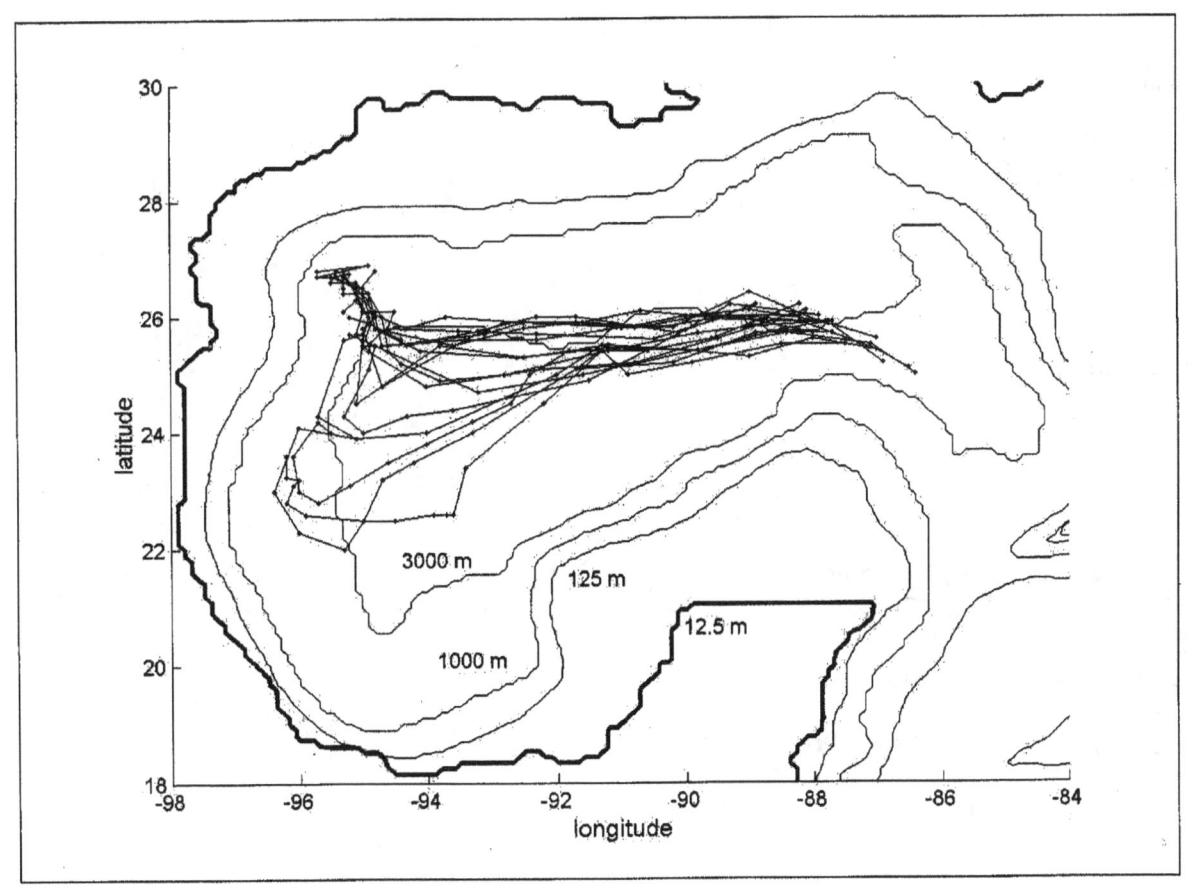

U.S. Department of the Interior
Minerals Management Service
Gulf of Mexico OCS Region

Cooperative Agreement
Coastal Marine Institute
Louisiana State University

OCS Study
MMS 2002-064

Coastal Marine Institute

Lagrangian Study of Circulation, Transport, and Vertical Exchange in the Gulf of Mexico

Authors

Susan E. Welsh
Masamichi Inoue

November 2002

Prepared under MMS Contract
14-35-0001-30660-19952
by
Coastal Marine Institute
Louisiana State University
Baton Rouge, Louisiana 70803

Published by

U.S. Department of the Interior
Minerals Management Service
Gulf of Mexico OCS Region

Cooperative Agreement
Coastal Marine Institute
Louisiana State University

DISCLAIMER

This report was prepared under contract between the Minerals Management Service (MMS) and Louisiana State University. This report has been technically reviewed by the MMS and approved for publication. Approval does not signify that the contents necessarily reflect the view and policies of the Service nor does mention of trade names or commercial products constitute endorsement or recommendation for use. It is, however, exempt from review and compliance with MMS editorial standards.

REPORT AVAILABILITY

Extra copies of the report may be obtained from the Public Information Office (MS 5034) at the following address:

U.S. Department of the Interior
Minerals Management Service
Gulf of Mexico OCS Region
Public Information Office (MS 5034)
1201 Elmwood Park Boulevard
New Orleans, Louisiana 70123-2394

Telephone Number: (504) 736-2519
1-800-200-GULF

CITATION

Suggested citation:

S.E. Welsh and M. Inoue. 2002. Langrangian study of the circulation, transport, and vertical exchange in the Gulf of Mexico: Final report. OCS Study MMS 2002-064. U.S. Dept. of the Interior, Minerals Management Service, Gulf of Mexico OCS Region, New Orleans, La. 51 pp.

ABSTRACT

The recent increased activity associated with offshore oil and gas exploration and production in the outer continental shelf and slope regions of the northern Gulf of Mexico (GOM) calls for a better understanding of the ocean circulation in these regions and the potential environmental effects of those activities. Safe operation of offshore facilities during exploration and production is required for the protection of human life and the marine environment. Moving into deep water places the oil and gas operations closer to strong surface-intensified currents associated with the Loop Current (LC) and LC rings. Sub-surface current measurements over the northern continental slope provide evidence of vigorous currents and Topographic Rossby Waves. In the deep GOM below 1000 m, vertically homogeneous currents are observed to intensify near the bottom. Understanding how these deep energetic currents and eddies interact with the bottom topography is important to ensure that deepwater activities are safe and environmentally sound. Three other considerations in the mining of deep sea mineral resources are (1) the transport of material by deep currents in both the horizontal and vertical; (2) mixing and ventilation of deep water; and (3) the residence time of water in the deep GOM.

The first goal of this project was to realistically reproduce the observed upper-layer circulation features of the GOM using a primitive-equation, numerical ocean model. The model features high vertical resolution and seasonally-varying inflow through the Yucatan Channel. Special attention was given to simulating the 3-dimensional structure of the LC and LC rings, which dominate the circulation in the eastern GOM. Lagrangian methods were used to analyze the trajectories of tens of thousands of inert tracer particles in an effort to characterize the three-dimensional circulation and transport pathways in the GOM. Specific goals were to identify regions where vertical exchanges may occur and what processes are responsible for ventilation of the deep water. The exchange of particles across density surfaces occurs mainly beneath the LC in the eastern GOM, in the northwestern region where LC rings spin-down, and near steep slopes. During the process of ring separation, particles were observed to slowly spiral upward in the water column within the lower layer. The descent of particles occurs in the eastern GOM as cold, fresh water cascades over the sill beneath the Yucatan Current and flows northward along the Florida Escarpment before turning westward. There was little communication between the eastern and central regions of the GOM across 88°W below the surface layer. Tracer particles in the deep GOM to the west of 88°W are observed to continually circulate in a generally cyclonic direction, indicating a mean cyclonic drift in the deep water. Analysis of individual particle paths and comparison of those paths to the model circulation has provided information on the possible mechanisms for exchange of surface and deep water.

TABLE OF CONTENTS

LIST OF FIGURES

LIST OF TABLES

CHAPTER 1

INTRODUCTION

1.1   Deep Water Research

Offshore oil and gas exploration and production in the Gulf of Mexico (GOM) has moved seaward into water depths greater than 300 m, creating a need for new technologies. The recent success of the deepwater projects has resulted in a commitment by industry to continue exploring the outer continental shelf and slope for mineral resources and to develop and improve technology for safe operation of deepwater facilities. Detailed understanding of the ocean environment on the slope region is essential in order to assess the adequacy of the existing regulations and environmental impacts of all facets of deepwater exploration and production. The deep GOM is also ecologically interesting. Along the continental slope there is an abundance of benthic communities associated with numerous hydro-carbon seeps. Moreover, there may be distinct habitats that are zoned according to depth and it is not understood what controls the diversity in the deep sea (Carney 1997). The goal of this study was to characterize the transport, mixing, and ventilation processes in deep water in order to assess the environmental impacts of exploration and production on deep-sea communities.

The following MMS field programs have provided information about the general circulation and eddy fields along the shelf and slope from the U.S.-Mexican border to the west Florida Shelf: Louisiana/Texas Physical Oceanography Program (LATEX), the Northeastern Gulf of Mexico Physical Oceanography Program, the Northeastern Gulf of Mexico Coastal and Marine Ecosystem Program, GulfCet I & II, and the DeSoto Eddy Intrusion Study. The relevance of these observational programs to a modeling study of deep water is in the model verification process. The GOM can be considered as a two-layer system in which the behavior of the upper layer anticyclones and lower layer eddies are coupled and the bottom bathymetry can influence the path of the ring in the upper layer through feedback from the lower layer (Hurlburt and Thompson 1982). A modeling study that aims to describe vertical exchanges and horizontal advection should accurately represent the upper layer processes, as well as the deep oceanographic environment.

The GOM is a semi-enclosed sea with maximum depths of approximately 3400 m in the eastern portion and 3700 m in the western portion. The surface waters of the GOM have been studied in great detail. In comparison, there is very little information about the circulation below 1000 m. Direct current measurements were rare (e. g., Pequegnat 1972; Hamilton 1990) until recently (Wiseman and Walker, 2001, unpublished data; Inoue et al. 2002; Hamilton and Lugo-Fernandez 2001). Also limited attention has been focused on the deep circulation in the GOM by the modeling community. Although the deep water of the GOM below the deepest sill depth is completely isolated from outside, it is well-ventilated (Buerkert 1997; Berberian and Cantillo 1999). Renewal of deep water should take place only via vertical exchange of water with the water above the sill depth. Several modeling studies of the GOM have indicated the presence of energetic deep vortices (e.g., Hurlburt and Thompson 1982; Indest 1992; Sturges et al. 1993; Welsh and Inoue 2000). Generation of deep vortices, interaction of deep vortices with bottom topography (Vidal et al. 1994), and the spin down of upper layer anticyclones (Flierl and Mied 1985; Schmitz and Vastano 1976) appear to play an important role in the vertical exchange of water in the GOM.

1.2   The General Circulation

The Loop Current (LC) enters the GOM from the Caribbean Sea through the Yucatan Channel (sill depth of approximately 1900 m) and exits through the southern Straits of Florida (sill depth of about 800 m). The upper-layer circulation in the eastern GOM is dominated by boundary fluctuations of the LC and the separation of anticyclonic eddies, referred to herein as LC rings. Estimates of the ring separation period have been changing as more data has become available. The previously published range was between 6 and 17 months (Sturges 1994; Vukovich 1995), and estimates of the primary and secondary separation modes are 8-9 months and 13-14 months, respectively. The most recent analysis of 34 rings from 1973 to 1999 includes new or revised data with ring separation periods as 3 and 5 months. Peaks in a histogram of this data occur at 6 months and 9 months with a broad peak at 11 months (Sturges and Leben 2000). The mean separation period during this 27-year record is close to 9.5 months, which is somewhat shorter than an earlier estimate of 11 months (Vukovich 1995).

The three-dimensional structure of LC rings has been reported by several authors (Elliot 1982; Vukovich and Crissman 1986; Lewis and Kirwan 1987; and Cooper et al. 1990). LC rings have average diameters in the eastern GOM of 300-400 km and surface current speeds can reach 2 ms^{-1}. The strong currents associated with the rings are observed to penetrate to depths of 700-800m. A core of high salinity Subtropical Underwater (>36.6 PSU at 22.5°C) is found in the LC rings at depths of 150-250 m. LC rings migrate westward with an average translation speed of 4 km/day and have a typical life span of one year. As a ring migrates westward, the following changes are observed: there is a shoaling of the isotherms relative to the surrounding water, the subsurface salinity maximum degrades, the lateral extent of the rings decreases, and there is a substantial decrease in peak swirl velocities.

Vukovich and Crissman (1986) analyzed GOES and ocean infrared satellite images collected over a 12-year period and concluded that there were three main LC ring paths. The LC rings following the predominant path (path 1) reach the western wall at around 22°N and then move northward. All ring paths in this 12-year study terminate in the northwestern corner, sometimes referred to as the "eddy graveyard". Kirwan et al. (1988) described the westward migration of two LC rings using satellite-tracked drifters. Both of these rings migrated toward the southwest and reached the western boundary near 22.8°N and eventually moved northward.

After reaching the Mexican-Texas slope there are several scenarios as to the fate of LC rings. Hamilton et al. (1999) follow the paths of ten eddies in the western Gulf using ARGOS-tracked drifters and hydrographic surveys. The authors conclude that there are no preferred LC ring paths in the main basin or that LC rings move in a preferred direction once reaching the western slope. Sturges et al. (1993) estimated that LC rings decay rapidly once they reach the western boundary (~70 days) and do not contribute to a western boundary current, whereas (Vidal et al. 1999) state that the contribution of anticyclonic vorticity from rings is a major factor in the maintenance of a western boundary current. The stalling of LC eddies in the far northwestern portion of the GOM contributes to a cyclonic gyre on the Louisiana-Texas shelf as well as the existence of an eastward current that runs along the shelf break to the Mississippi Delta (Oey 1995).

1.3   Numerical Simulation of Gulf of Mexico Circulation

Several different types of numerical models have been used to model circulation in GOM. Since the pioneering modeling study of circulation in GOM by Hurlburt and Thompson (1980, 1982) the following models have been implemented: Princeton Ocean Model, Modular Ocean Model, Naval Research Laboratory global layer-model, Miami Isopycnic Coordinate Model. Those models use either a limited-domain or a larger-domain. The use of a limited-domain usually requires the specification of inflow as well as outflow representing the LC and the Florida Current, respectively. Under a larger-domain, circulation within GOM is modeled as part of a much larger model domain, such as the entire North Atlantic, or even a global circulation model. The use of a larger-domain alleviates the need to specify flow into and out of GOM. However, the model resolution suffers due to the increased computational efforts required.

Welsh (1996) and Inoue and Welsh (1997) used the Modular Ocean Model to describe both the surface and deep circulation in the GOM using a 0.1° grid. The model was able to simulate many features of the observed upper-layer seasonal circulation including the volume transport through the Yucatan Channel, the western boundary current in the GOM, upwelling on the Campeche Bank, and the seasonal cyclonic circulation in the Campeche Bay. In addition, many of the observed features of LC rings were simulated in the model, including their initial size, mean swirl speed, migration speed, characteristic migration paths (Vukovich and Crissman 1986), and life span.

Model studies of Sturges et al. (1993) and Welsh and Inoue (2000) indicate that deep motions in the GOM are highly coherent in the vertical from nearly 1300 m all the way to the bottom, as recorded by deep current meter moorings (Hamilton 1990). Welsh and Inoue (2000) observed that an anticyclone-cyclone pair forms in the eastern GOM beneath the LC as a ring is separating from the LC. Deep cyclones and deep anticyclone-cyclone pairs have also been identified in other modeling studies of the GOM circulation (Hurlburt and Thompson 1982; Indest 1992; Sturges et al. 1993). The following similarities are noted for these three studies: (1) an anticyclone-cyclone pair, which Hurlburt and Thompson (1982) refer to as a 'modon (Stern 1975)', is generated in the lower layer during the formation of LC rings; (2) during westward migration, the axis of the modon is oriented close to the direction of propagation of the ring with the anticyclone leading; and (3) the leading lower-layer anticyclone weakens relative to the trailing cyclone as the modon propagates westward (except for experiment 2 of Hurlburt and Thompson (1982) which featured an upper layer inflow directed 27° west of normal and no lower layer inflow). Hurlburt and Thompson (1982) reported that in the case with idealized bathymetry, the modon is confined to the abyssal plain and is steered by the bathymetry, which is also evident in Welsh and Inoue (2000).

The connection between the migration of LC rings in the upper layer and the deep circulation of the GOM has been observed in several numerical models (Hurlburt and Thompson 1982; Sturges et al. 1993; and Welsh and Inoue 2000). Cushman-Roisin et al. (1990) investigated the generation of deep cyclone-anticyclone pairs in conjunction with the westward migration of surface anticyclones for a two-layer system with a flat bottom and a rigid lid. A depression forms in the vertical interface between an anticyclonic eddy in the surface layer and the deeper layer with respect to the surrounding fluid. The relative vorticity of the lower layer is higher beneath the eddy than beneath the surrounding fluid, and as the eddy migrates westward on a â-plane, the lower layer acquires anticyclonic relative vorticity beneath the eddy and cyclonic relative vorticity behind the eddy. The result is an eddy pair in the lower layer with the leading anticyclone beneath the surface vortex and a trailing cyclone (Cushman-Roisin et al. 1990).

The existence and fate of lower layer modons coupled to upper layer surface intensified vortices over variable topography has recently been examined using analytical models (Reznik and Sutyrin 2001; Sutyrin 2001). The effect of the cross-slope drift of an upper layer vortex is to create dipolar gyres in the lower layer. Feedback from the lower layer modon on the upper layer vortex creates additional westward propagation along the isobaths (Sutyrin 2001). If the slope of the interface between the upper and lower layer vortices is comparable to the slope of the topography, then the gyres in the lower layer lose their mirror symmetry and the cyclonic gyre strengthens relative to the anticyclonic gyre (Sutyrin 2001).

CHAPTER 2

OVERVIEW OF NUMERICAL SIMULATIONS

2.1   Numerical Model Configuration

The Modular Ocean Model version 1.1 (Pacanowski et al. 1991), a three-dimensional, primitive-equation, numerical model, which has evolved from the Bryan-Cox model (Bryan 1969; Cox 1984), was chosen for this study. This model is ideal for this project because the effects of bottom topography and the resolution of eddy dynamics are both important in the GOM. The model grid is derived from the ETOP05 world topography data set. The bathymetric values are linearly interpolated to 0.1° and smoothed to prevent topographically induced 2Äx noise in the numerical solution. The model domain extends from 98.0°W to 72.0°W and from 15.0°N to 31.0°N. The model grid has lateral dimensions of 280 by 161. There are 20 levels in the vertical with a maximum depth of 3850 m. The use of evenly spaced vertical levels is preferred to reduce the error in the finite difference formulation of the vertical velocity. Greater resolution is needed near the surface for more accurate representation of the shelf bathymetry and to resolve the thermocline. Therefore the thickness of each of the upper 3 levels is 25 m, the lowest 10 levels are each 300-m thick, and the transition region represented by levels 4 through 10 gradually increases in depth. These depths are summarized in Table 1.

In order to achieve a realistic inflow condition, this model domain extends outside the GOM into a synthetic return flow region that links the Straits of Florida with the western Caribbean (Figure 1). The bathymetry in the return flow region is altered to allow flow exiting the GOM to re-circulate around Cuba and enter the GOM through the western Caribbean. The method of forcing the inflow is the same as has been implemented in previous modeling studies by Welsh (Inoue and Welsh 1997; Welsh and Inoue 2000).

The annual averages of the 3-D temperature and salinity fields used to initialize the model are derived from the Global Ocean Temperature and Salinity Data (NODC 1994). Level 1 temperature and salinity fields (vertically centered at a depth of 12.5 m) are restored to seasonal climatology with a relaxation time scale of 6 weeks. This surface boundary condition prevents the temperature and salinity in the surface layer from drifting away from the observed climatology. The surface wind stress field is derived from the Hellerman and Rosenstein (1983) normal monthly wind stress climatology. Wind stress is applied over the entire GOM and in the Caribbean to the west of the geostrophic forcing region, but no wind stress is applied over the return flow region. The wind stress field changes smoothly in time by linear interpolation at each time step.

A target value of 28 Sv is chosen to represent the annual-mean volume transport through the southern Straits of Florida. This target volume transport is based on published analyses of current meter measurements and cable-based transport measurements across each of the various channels that feed the Florida Current. Scientific Applications International Corporation (SAIC) (1992) estimated the annual-mean transport through the Florida Straits at 27°N to be 31.1 Sv and the combined annual-mean transport through the Old Bahama Channel and the Northwest Providence Channel to be 2.8 Sv. Subtracting the combined transports through these two

6

channels from the transport at 27°N results in an annual-mean transport through the southern Straits of Florida of 28.3 Sv. The widely accepted value for the volume transport of the Florida Current at 24°N is 30 Sv (Schmitz et al. 1992), which includes the 1.9 Sv flowing through the Old Bahama Channel measured by SAIC (1992).

Table 1

Depths of the Grid Levels in Meters

Grid level	DZ	DZT	DZW	DW
1	25.	12.5	25.	25.
2	25.	37.5	25.	50.
3	25.	62.5	25.	75.
4	31.25	87.5	37.5	106.25
5	43.75	125.	50.	150.
6	62.50	175.	75.	212.50
7	87.50	250.	100.	300.
8	125.	350.	150.	425.
9	175.	500.	200.	600.
10	250.	700.	300.	850.
11	300.	1000.	300.	1150.
12	300.	1300.	300.	1450.
13	300.	1600.	300.	1750.
14	300.	1900.	300.	2050.
15	300.	2200.	300.	2350.
16	300.	2500.	300.	2650.
17	300.	2800.	300.	2950.
18	300.	3100.	300.	3250.
19	300.	3400.	300.	3550.
20	300.	3700.	150.	3850.

DZ=height of T-grid boxes.
DZT=depth at the center of each T-grid box.
DZW=the distance between centers of T-grid boxes.
DW=depth at the bottom of each T-grid box.

The total volume flux through the Yucatan Channel is controlled by adding a constant to the u-component of velocity at each grid point within the geostrophic forcing region. During spin-up, this constant is increased by small increments until the annual average of the volume transport through the Yucatan Channel is equal to the target value. At least one year of spin-up time is needed for the model to adjust to changes in the target volume transport. The vertical shear of the Caribbean Current is created by relaxing the temperature and salinity along a north-south transect centered at 82.0°W in the geostrophic forcing region to the monthly climatology. A relaxation time scale of 6 weeks was used to produce flow through this transect that best approximated the observed geostrophic shear.

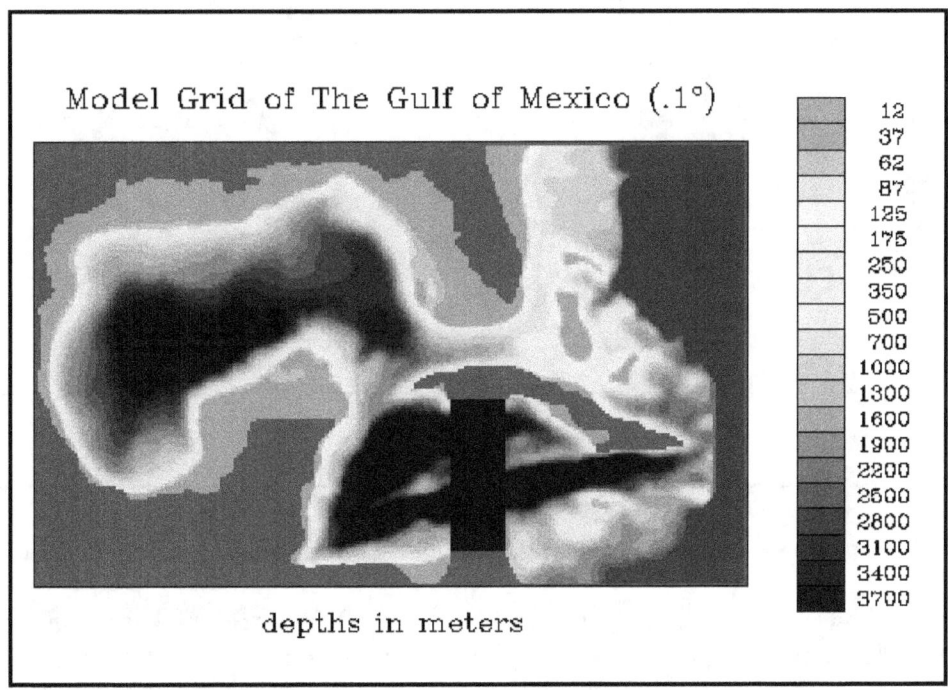

Figure 1. Model grid of the Gulf of Mexico.

Twelve-year cross-sectional averages of the *u*- and *v*-components of the inflow through the Yucatan Channel are presented in Figure 2. The core of the flow is concentrated near the surface on the western portion of the Channel. There is about 15 Sv of southward flow directed toward the Caribbean near the western Cuban Coast, as well as regions of southward flow (maximum 5 Sv) in the center of the channel near the bottom.

2.2   Particle Tracing Method

The Lagrangian technique of seeding and tracking tracer particles in the model is used to examine detailed transport and mixing processes and to identify the processes responsible for ventilation of the deep water. The model is seeded with large numbers of inert particles that drift freely within the model domain in response to the velocity field. Several different experiments were designed that feature different starting positions of the tracer particles that depend on the region or process that we are interested in. The positions of the tracers were recorded and later analyzed to identify characteristic flow paths and assess the effects of physical processes on the individual particles.

8

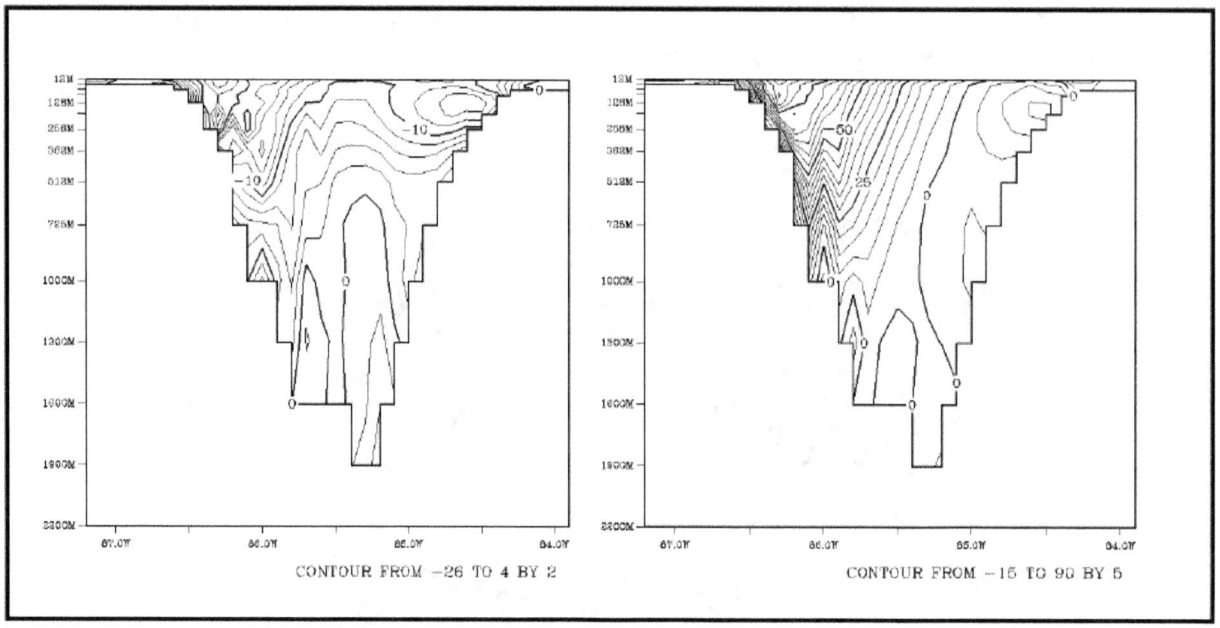

Figure 2. 12-year mean *u*- and *v*-components of velocity through the Yucatan Channel.

The method used to track the particles (Pacanowski 1996) features three-dimensional interpolation of each particle position at each time step followed by integration of the particle position in space using the three-dimensional components of velocity. Each particle is bounded within the space defined by the vertices given by the eight nearest surrounding model grid points. The indices of the deepest northeast corner of this bounding volume are recorded. The volume weights for linear interpolation of velocity at the vertices of the bounding volume to the particle position are computed. The velocity at the position of a particle is constructed by 3-D linear interpolation. The particle trajectory is integrated forward for one time and the bottom most northeast index of bounding volume is then updated. Any component of the trajectory is reset to its previous value if it crosses over to land, thereby simulating free slip conditions.

In addition to recording locations of particle positions, the model temperature, salinity, horizontal velocity, and stream function are saved at selected levels every 10 days and at every grid point every 30 days. Animations of the particle positions superimposed on the model flow fields were made to qualitatively assess the ability of the model to transport the tracer particles within oceanographic features. The method of integrating the particle positions in response to the model flow field appears to work extremely well.

2.3   Summary of Model Simulations

The model development and verification took place during the first 23 years of model integration. Changes and improvements were made to the model forcing, the variable viscosity, and the particle tracing methods. Five separate modeling experiments were made with different starting regions for the tracer particles. In each of these experiments the same restart file for the end of model year 23 is used, and the starting location of the tracers is changed. The first experiment was designed to provide information about how the deep water (below 2000 m) circulates and where the vertical exchange of fluid takes place. The model was seeded with 19,105 tracer particles at the center of all grid boxes from 2200 m to 3700 m. The particles were tracked for 12 model years (year 24 through year 35). The results of Experiment 1 were very insightful and are described in Section 4.2.

The next three experiments were designed to identify the regions and processes associated with the vertical exchange of fluid within the upper layer (0-1000 m). In Experiment 2, the top two layers (centered at 12.5 m and 37.5 m) were seeded with 28,294 tracer particles, which were tracked for six model years (year 24 through 29). A shortcoming of this experiment was that many particles were quickly flushed-out through the Florida Straits or into the Caribbean, and some particles became stranded in shallow water. Although many particles were eliminated from the system due to flushing or grounding, enough particles remained buoyant to make some interesting observations. The results of Experiment 2 are presented in section 4.3.

Experiment 3 was designed to see how much vertical exchange is taking place at the base of the mixed layer. This experiment featured a repeat of model years 24 through 26 with 18184 particles initially placed at the centers of levels 5 (128.125 m) and 6 (181.250 m). The results of Experiment 3 are described in section 4.4. Experiment 4 was designed to look at lateral circulation and vertical exchange processes at a depth of 1000 m (level 11). The model was initialized with 7606 tracer particles at the center of level 11 and model years 24 through 26 were again repeated. The results of Experiment 4 are described in Section 4.5.

The purpose of the final experiment, Experiment 5, was to learn about flow at fixed locations over time. The model was seeded with 116 particles at 2200 m (level 15), but only in water depths less than or equal to 2800 m (level 17). Every 4th grid box in both the north-south and east-west direction was initialized. We were primarily interested in particle trajectories directly over the slope. The particles were reset to their initial positions at the start of each month and their movement was recorded every 10 days for 30-day periods. For this experiment only model years 24 and 25 were repeated and the results are described in Section 4.6.

2.4 Model General Circulation

Many aspects of the general circulation of the GOM are reproduced in the output of this model. All of the features of the seasonal circulation that were generated in the previous 1/8° modeling study (Inoue and Welsh, 1997; Welsh and Inoue, 2000) are again observed in this study. Features such as the spring/summer upwelling on the Campeche Bank and the late summer/fall cyclonic circulation in the Campeche Bay are observed, but are not discussed in this report. A description of the general behavior of the LC, LC ring separation, and LC ring westward migration are included because the vertical motions observed in the model are highly correlated with the LC and LC ring behavior. The separation, life span, and disappearance of rings S1 through S8 were described by analyzing plots of level 1 temperature contours and velocity vectors at 10-day intervals. A summary of these observations is presented in Table 2.

Year 24 begins with a ring (S0) in the western GOM centered near 25°N and 94°W and the LC is centered at 86.6°W and 25.2°N. By day 90 a new ring (S1) has completely separated from the LC and is centered at 89°W and 26.2°N. Ring S0 reaches the northwest corner and is centered at 26°N, 95.25°W on day 150. On day 170 rings S0 and S1 begin to exchange fluid around their peripheries and by day 200 the two rings appear to have completely merged.

Table 2

Life Histories of Nine LC Rings that Separated during Model Years 24 through 28

Ring	Separation between (year/day)	Time separations (weeks)	Reach 91°W 91°W (year/day)	Time to reach (weeks)	Reach Eddy Graveyard (year/day)	Life Span (weeks)
S1			24 / 140	[180]	24 / 270	320
S2	24 / 90		24 / 320	[210]	25 / 160	490
S3	24 / 240	[150]	25 / 170	[190]	25 / 280	400
S4	25 / 120	[240]	25 / 360	[220]		340
S5	25 / 260	[140]	26 / 220	[200]	26 / 330	300
S6	26 / 150	[250]	27 / 60	[180]	27 / 200	340
S7	26 / 350	[200]	27 / 240	[220]	27 / 340	310
S8	27 / 160	[170]	28 / 100	[200]	28 / 190	400
S9	28 / 50	[250]	28 / 300	[200]		
	28 / 220	[170]				

average life span = 346 days; average time to reach 91°W = 200 days
minimum separation interval = 4.6 months; maximum separation interval = 8.3 months
average separation interval = 196.25 days

Ring S2 has completely separated from the LC by day 240 and ring S1 has reached the northwest corner by day 270. Ring S2 becomes very elongated in a northeast-southwest direction at 92.6°W and 24.5°N near day 360 and has split apart by day 10 of year 25. The southern portion of S2 moves toward the southwest until it reaches the slope and then moves rapidly northward. Meanwhile the northern portion moves westward and eventually merges with its other half on day 70 of year 25. Ring S3 separates on day 120 of year 25. Ring S2 reaches the northwest corner by day 160. Rings S2 and S3 begin to merge on day 170 of year 25 and the surface velocity signature of ring S2 vanishes by day 210.

The LC stays confined to the southeastern GOM during the formation of ring S4. The center of circulation of ring S4 at the time of separation on day 260 of year 25 is located at 87.2°W and 25.5°N. By comparison, ring S3 had a center of circulation near 89°W and 26.2°N at the time of separation. The LC reformed much deeper into the northeastern GOM after separation of ring S3 than after the separation of ring S4 (Figure 3). The interesting thing to note is that ring S4 separated only 140 days after ring S3, while ring S5 separated 250 days after ring S3. The length of time between consecutive shedding events is positively correlated with the position of the LC after the first ring has shed. If the LC reforms far to the south, then the interval before the next eddy shedding is relatively long. Whereas if the LC extends far into the GOM after a ring has separated, then the interval between shedding events is shorter.

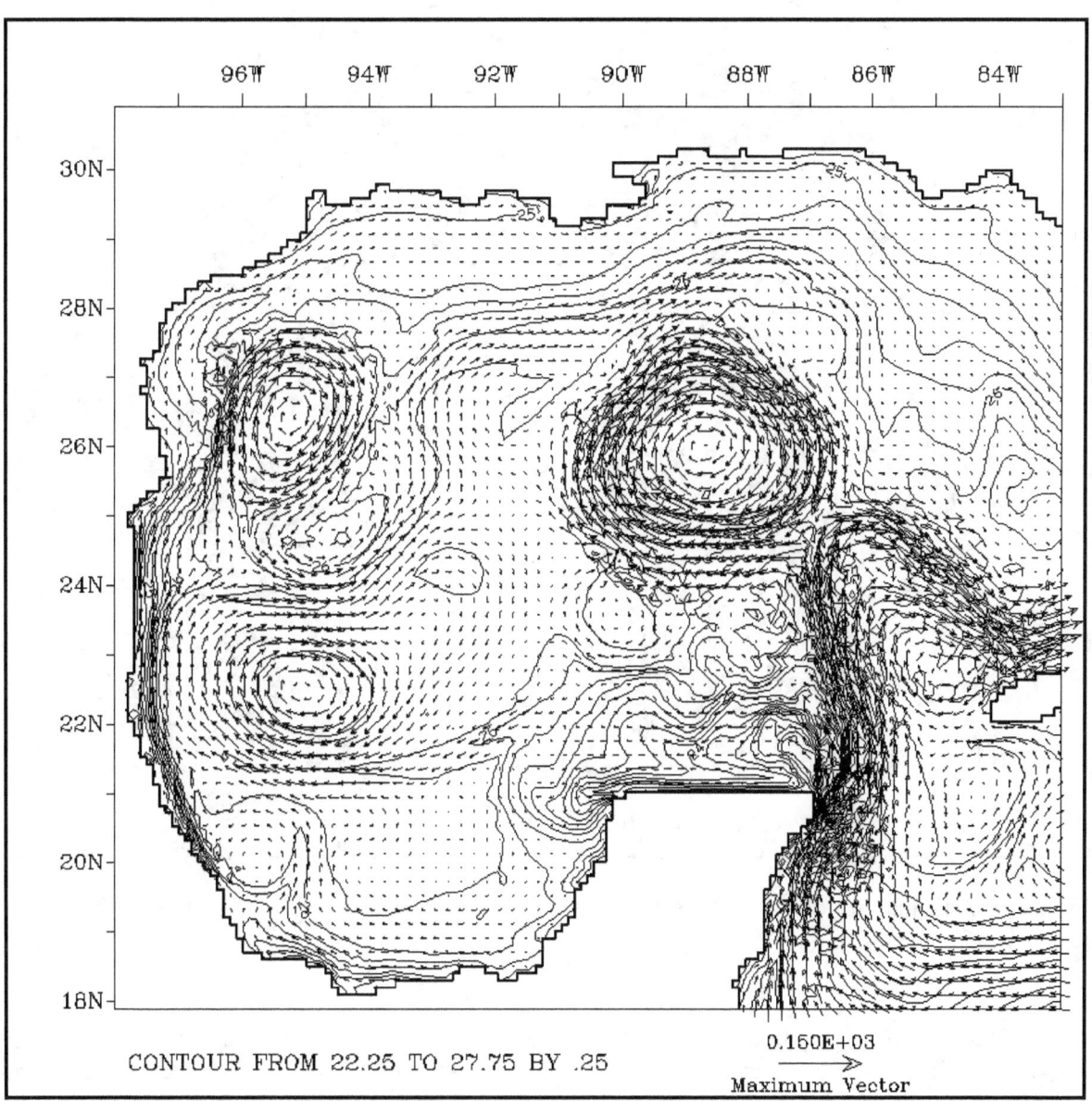

Figure 3A. Temperature and velocity fields at level 1 (12.5 m) during the shedding of Ring S3 on year 25, day 260.

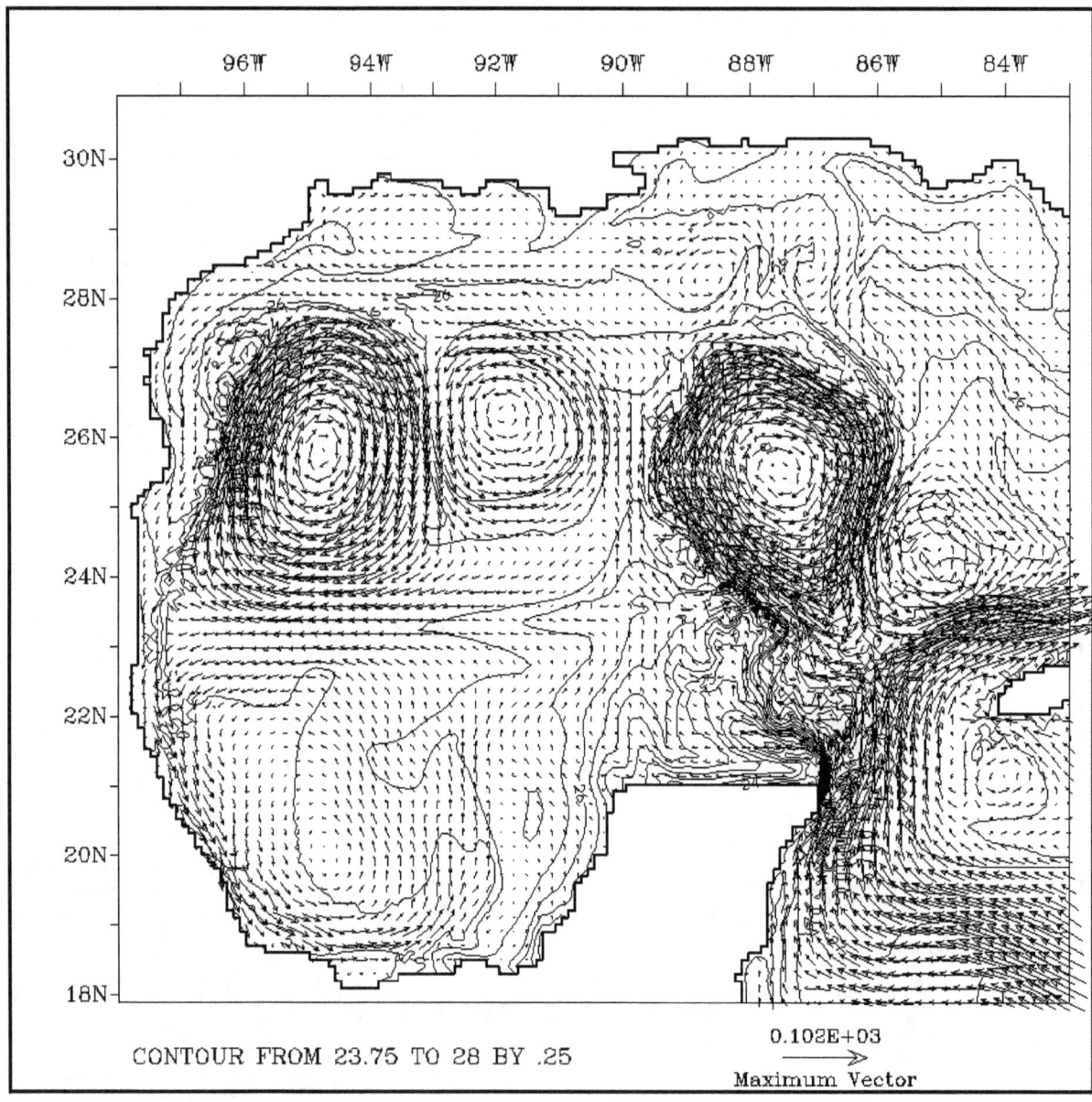

CONTOUR FROM 23.75 TO 28 BY .25

0.102E+03

Maximum Vector

Figure 3B. Temperature and velocity fields at level 1 (12.5 m) during the shedding of Ring S4 on year 26, day 150.

The time at which model LC rings become detached from the LC is determined by visual inspection of the surface velocity fields, as well as time series analysis of model temperature and velocity at selected locations. A histogram of separation intervals was constructed from the 27 shedding events over a 15-year model simulation (Figure 4). The criterion for a LC rings to have separated is for the circulation around the rings at the surface to be all or mostly closed.

13

Therefore, the moment that a ring has just separated is somewhat subjective, but the error is within ~15 model days. The minimum, maximum, and average separation interval that were observed during years 24 through 38 were 4.7 months, 8.3 months and 6.5 months, respectively. A time series of model velocity at 12.5 m, 25.5°N, 87°W for years 24 through 28 was compared to the timing of separation of rings S1 through S9. The minimum in north-south velocity occurs at the time of each ring separation to within ~20 days. A power spectrum was computed for this 15-year velocity time series (Figure 5). The peaks found at 4.5, 4.75, 6.5, and 8.3 are within the range of the model separation intervals. Smaller peaks are found at 9.5 and 14 months, but there is very little energy at 12 months (.055). The spectrum at lower frequencies (longer than 8.3 months/cycle) varies somewhat depending on the geographic location of the time series.

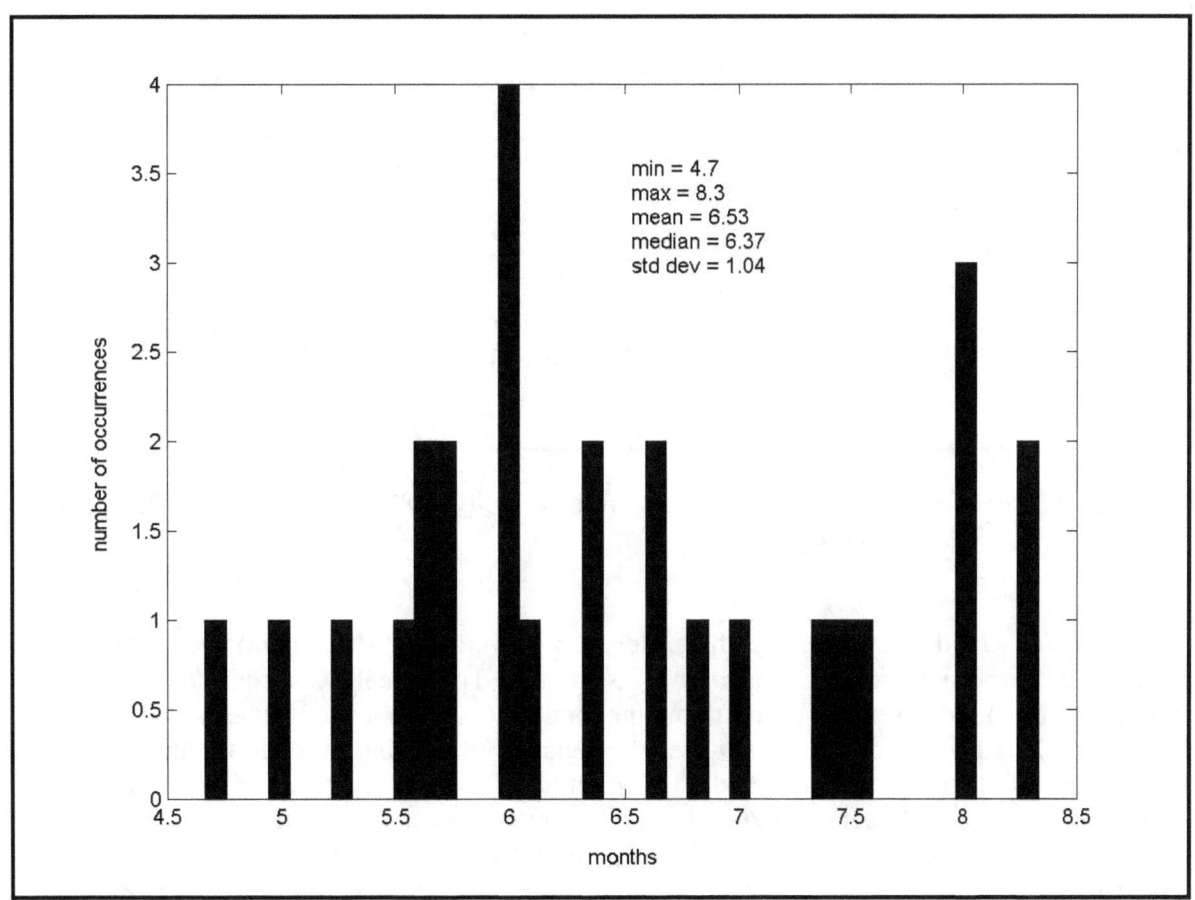

Figure 4. Histogram of 27 model LC ring separation intervals.

14

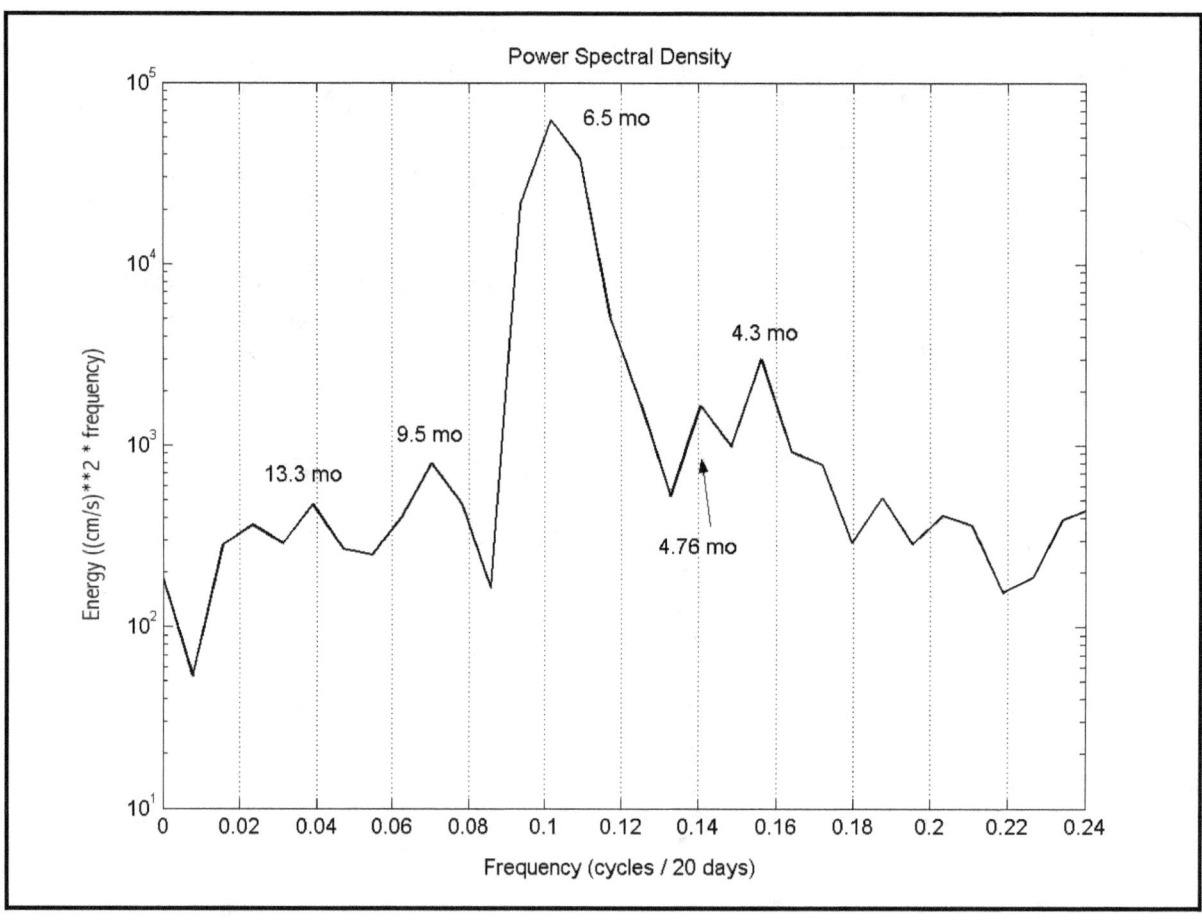

Figure 5. Power spectral density of *v*-component of velocity at 87°W, 25.5°N, and 12.5 m for model years 24 through 38.

The observed mean eddy shedding interval of 9.5 months [Sturges and Leben 2000] is larger than the mean model ring separation by 3 months. The model LC sheds eddies at the high frequency end of the observed spectrum, but the model LC does not shed eddies on time scales longer than 250 days. A difference between the behavior of LC ring formation in the model and the real world is that each time the model LC penetrates into the northeastern GOM, a ring separation takes place. In actuality, the LC can penetrate far into the eastern and sometimes the central GOM without shedding an eddy for many months. The LC penetrated far into the GOM and nearly shed an eddy in late fall 2000 and again in January 2001 before Millenium eddy completely separated and began to migrate westward in March/April 2001. LC rings have also been observed to separate and then rejoin the LC, which never occurs in the model.

The paths of the 16 model LC rings to separate during model years 24 through 32 are presented in Figure 6. These paths are determined by plotting the center of circulation of each ring in the top level (centered at 12.5m) every 10-30 days after the ring has completely detached from the LC. The center of each ring passes between 25°N and 26°N at 88°W, after which their

15

paths diverge. The majority of rings migrated almost directly westward, although five of the 16 rings migrated toward the southwest and were south of 24°N when they reached 95°W. Once in the far western GOM, most rings then moved northward along the slope into the 'eddy graveyard', which has its center at approximately 26.5°and 95°W. The eddy graveyard is the termination point for nearly all ring paths in this modeling study, other GOM modeling studies (Hurlburt and Thompson, 1982; Sturges et al., 1993; Oey, 1995), and observational studies of LC rings (Vukovich and Crissman, 1986). After LC rings enter the eddy graveyard, they continue to decrease in lateral size and swirl velocities. Also as the rings spin-down, the vertical displacement of the isotherms decreases and the sub-surface salinity maxima erodes. Only two of these16 model rings had completely dissipated before a new ring arrived, whereas the rest of the older rings were eventually absorbed by new rings.

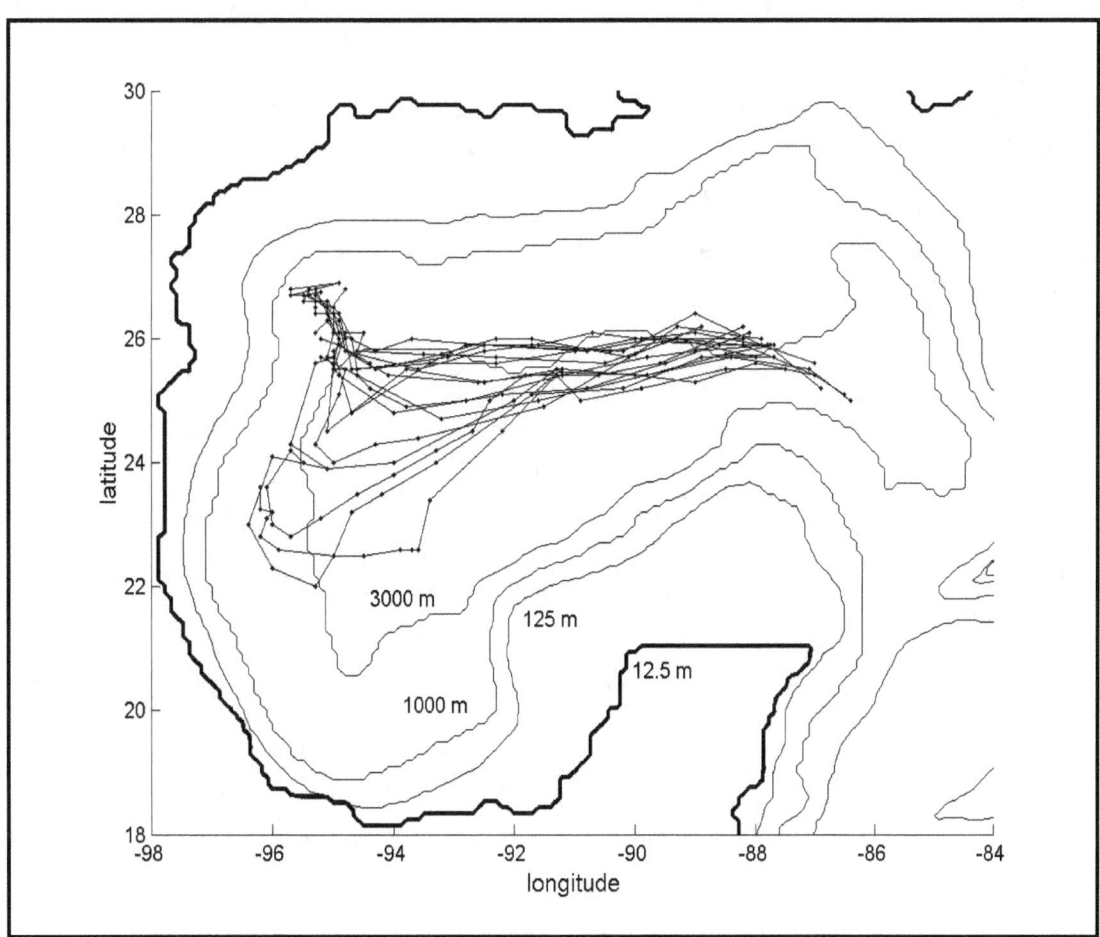

Figure 6. Paths of 16 LC rings observed during model years 24 through 32.

Vukovich and Crissman (1986) examined 12-years of National Oceanic and Atmospheric Administration (NOAA) infrared imagery and Geostationary Operational Environmental Satellite (GOES) data for the purpose of tracking the centers of warm core rings in the GOM. Nine long-term ring paths, a few short-term paths, and several isolated locations of ring centers were compared to determine the characteristic migration paths of LC rings. Six of the long-term paths were directed toward the southwest, two were directed toward the west, and one was observed to remain in the eddy graveyard for eight months in a region roughly centered at 94.5°W and 26.5°N. Several of the isolated ring centers also indicated a more generally westward migration. The model ring paths were in very good agreement with the observations. Most of the model rings followed a generally westward path, oriented along the 3000-m isobath, although five model rings were observed to follow a southwestward path. None of the model rings moved to the south after reaching the western slope, in agreement with the characteristic LC ring paths described by Vukovich and Crissman (1986) which converged in the northwestern GOM.

Hamilton et al. (1999) analyzed the paths of ten LC rings in the western GOM and determined that LC rings do not follow any preferred paths as they migrate westward and can move north or south after reaching the western slope. At least six of the ten rings analyzed by Hamilton et al. (1999) (C6, T, U, V, W and Y) were observed in the northwestern GOM (north of 25°N and west of 95°W) at some time during their life span. Hamilton et al. (1999) noted that the presence of lower slope cyclones in the northern GOM and the absorption of older, fossil LC rings influence the westward migration of LC rings.

CHAPTER 3

RESULTS OF PARTICLE TRACING EXPERIMENTS

3.1   Experiment 1: Bottom Water Tracer Particle Release

The model was seeded below 2000 m with 19,105 inert particles that drift freely within the model domain in response to the velocity field (Figure 7). Every ocean grid box at levels 15 through 20 (depths 2200 m through 3700 m) was seeded with a single particle. The positions of the tracers were recorded every 10 days for 16 model years (from the beginning of model year 24 through the end of model year 39). Groups of particles are referred to by their initial geographic locations: west, central and east.

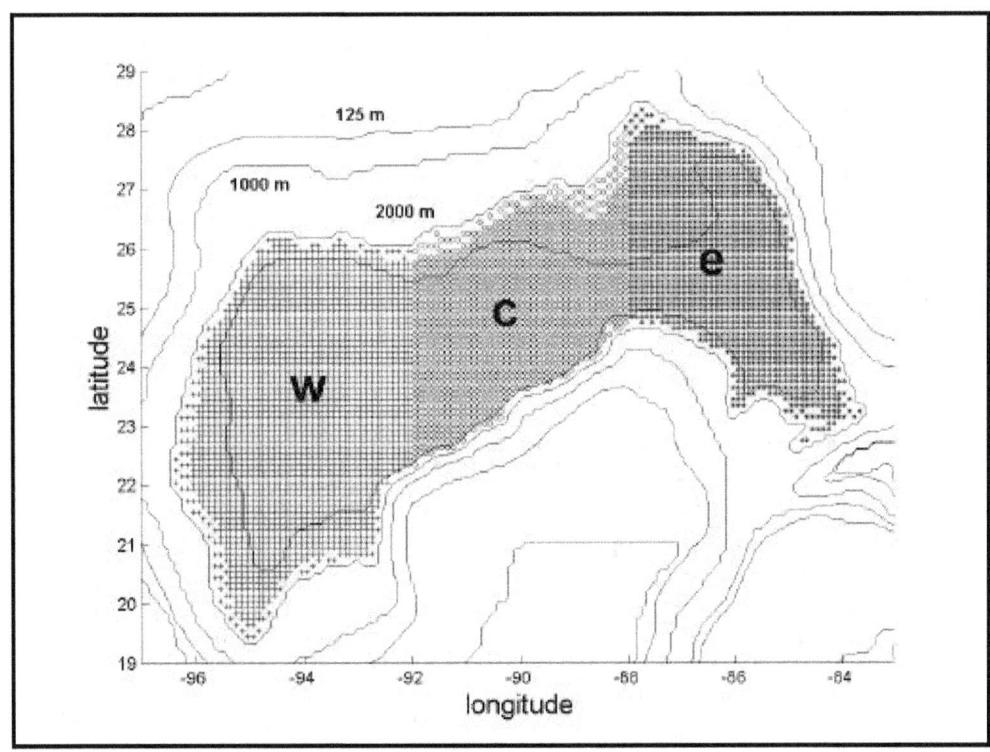

Figure 7. Plan view of initial starting locations at 2200 m for tracer particles in Experiment 1. The bold letters identify the starting regions as west (W), central (C), and east (E).

The percentages of all particles to rise above specified levels over a 16-year simulation are presented in Figure 8. Particles rose above 2000 m within the first year after initialization, 1000 m in year 27, and 500 m in year 30. The percentages of particles to rise above 2000 m, 1000 m, and 500 m according to starting locations are presented in Figure 9. Particles from the

18

east group rose most rapidly to all levels. Particles from the central and west groups rose above 2000 m at nearly the same rate, but the number of particles to rise above 1000 m from the west group was very small. The curves appear to level off because the supply of particles decreases in each region with time.

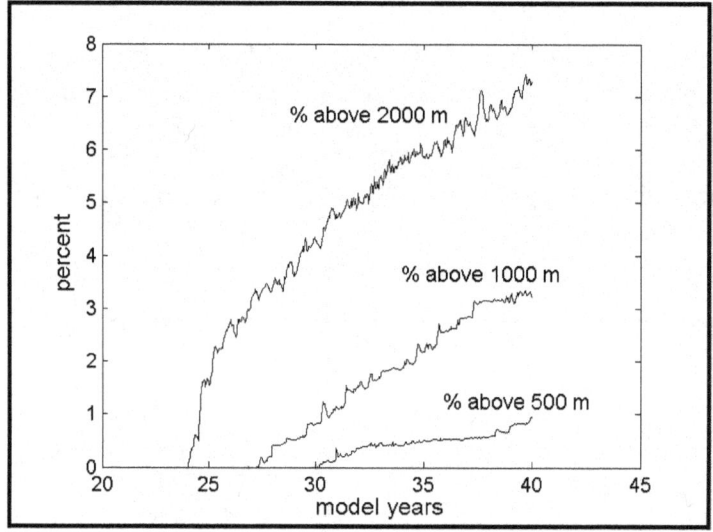

Figure 8. Percentages of particles to ascend above specified depth levels during the 16-year model simulation.

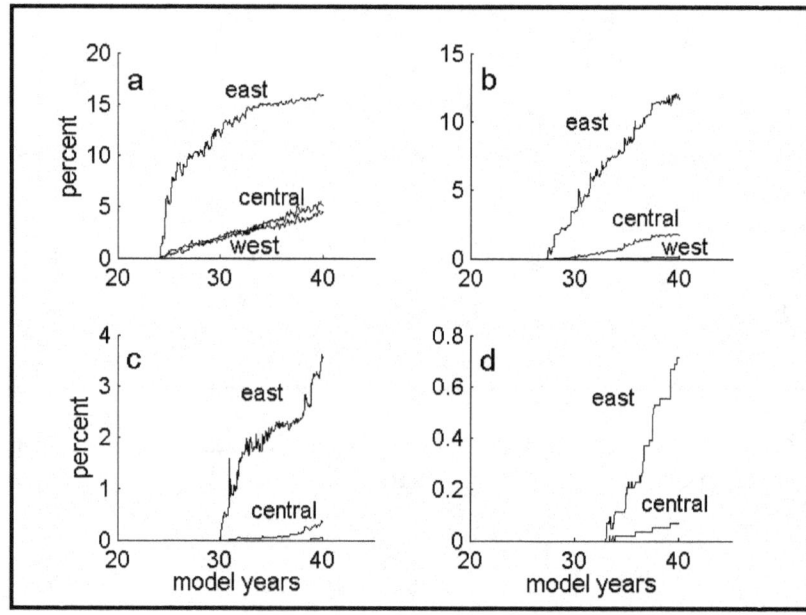

Figure 9. Percentages of all particles to ascend to (a) 2000 m, (b) 1000 m, (c) 500 m, and (d) 200 m according to starting location.

   Although the particle tracing method implemented in the model prevented the particles from entering the land using a free slip condition, the particles were not prevented from occasionally becoming stranded. If a particle became trapped in a grid box that was bounded on the two adjacent sides and the bottom by land, then the particle may remain there indefinitely or may become free again. The stranding of particles was observed in the visual analysis of particle tracks. The actual percentage of particles that became stranded in these experiments was not computed, but appeared to be very small.

   The lateral movement of the particles according to starting region over the 16-year simulation was also recorded. The longitude-depth projection of all particles at the end of the 15-year simulation and the projection of just those particles that were initially at 2200 m is presented in Figure 10. The particles tend to be segregated into regions east and west of 88°W. Particles mixed freely in the western and central portions, but were cut-off from mixing with the eastern portion. 9.11% of particles initially east of 88°W (blue) were located west of 88°W after 15 years and 8.71% of particles initially west of 88°W (red and green) were located to the east of 88°W after 15 years. 90.49% of all particles initially in the west and central portions (red and green) remained west of 88°W at depths below 1500m. Only 77.0% of eastern particles (blue) remained east of 88°W at depths below 1500m. These percentages indicate that there is little exchange of water across 88°W in the deep layer and that vertical exchange with the upper layer is occurring predominantly in the eastern basin. The lack of exchange between basins has been observed by Weatherly using PALACE floats at 1000 m depth (personnel communication, 2001) and by Lugo-Fernandez et al. (2001) from analysis of surface drifters in the GOM. The geographic restriction of tracer particles to the deep western basin is exemplified by the paths of particles 1007 and 4005, which is discussed in detail later in this chapter.

   By tracking individual particles, it can be seen that the upward motion of particles from below 2000 m to above 1000 m occurs almost exclusively in the ring separation region in the eastern GOM. Individual particles are observed to spiral upward with each separation of a new ring from the LC. Particle 16019 moves upward in a spiral that covers a lateral area of approximately 2° by 2° until the particle reaches 1000 m in year 27 (Figure 11). The circulation directly beneath the LC fluctuates between anticyclonic and cyclonic (Welsh and Inoue 2000) therefore the direction of rotation of the particle can change. Particle 19106 completed one and a half cyclonic rotations during year 25, and during year 26 particle 16109 completed two anticyclonic rotations. In year 28, particle 16019 was entrained in the LC at a depth of about 1000 m and the lateral excursion of the particle increased as the particle completed nearly two anticyclonic rotations. There is a direct correlation between the north-south excursion of particle 16109 and the ring separation index, which is defined as the water temperature at 87°W, 25.5°N and 125 m depth (Figure 12). In Year 27 the positive correlation of the particle's latitude with the ring separation index shifts and becomes negative in years 28 and 29 when the particle is entrained in the Loop Current. In the second half of year 29, a ring separates from the Loop Current and transports particle 16019 into the western GOM where it stagnates on the Mexican slope in year 30.

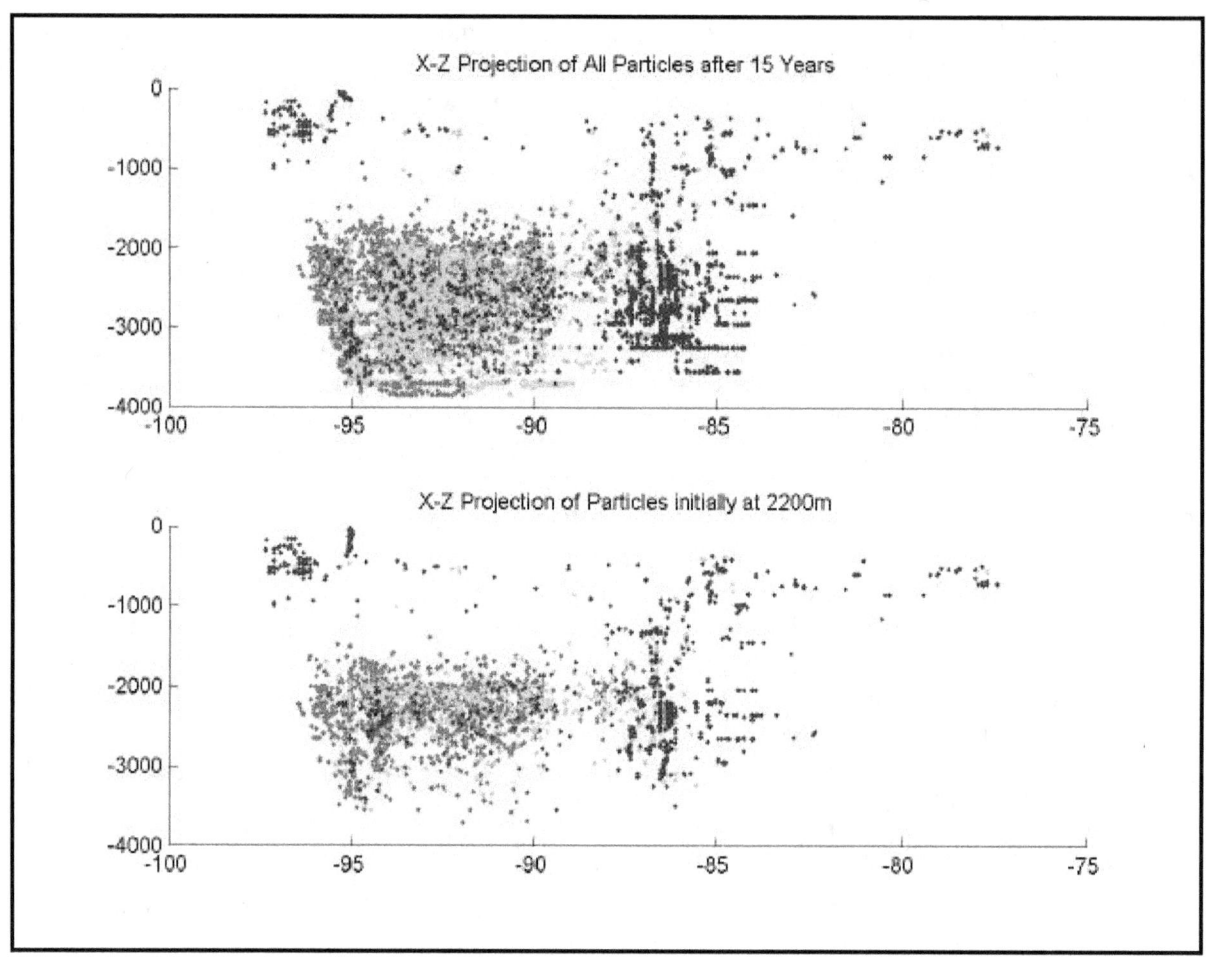

Figure 10. X-Z projection of particles according to starting location. Blue for particles initially east of 88°W, green for particles initially between 88°W and 92°W, and red for particles initially west of 92°W.

21

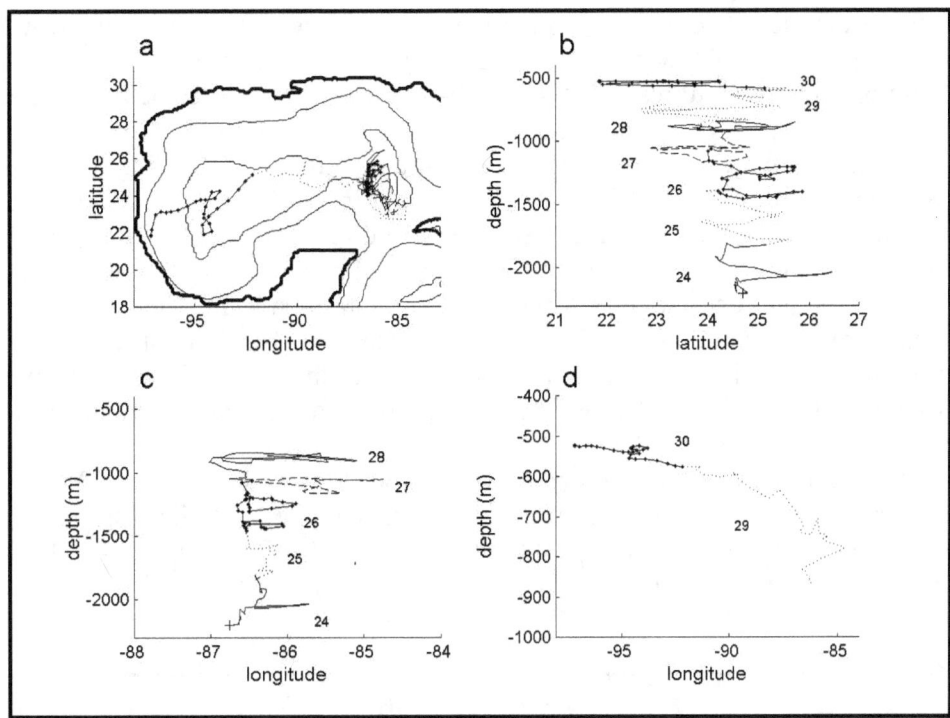

Figure 11. Path of particle 16019: (a) plan view for years 24-30, (b) latitude-depth projection for years 24-30, (c) longitude-depth projection while 16019 was in the eastern basin, and (d) longitude-depth projection after 16019 became entrained in Ring S9.

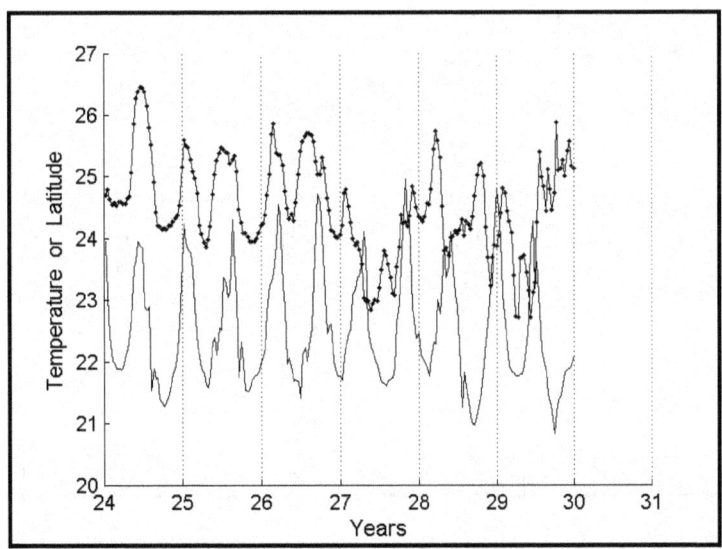

Figure 12. Time series of particle 16019 latitude (dotted) and temperature at 87°W, 25.5°N, 128 m.

22

Another example of particle movement in the deep eastern portion of the GOM is demonstrated by particle 17976, which was tracked for the entire 15 years (Figure 13). Particle 17976 took almost nine years to reach 500 m, during which time the particle made tight spirals in the eastern basin. The spirals became wider in the east-west direction from 1000 m to nearly 400 m in year 33 (Figure 13C) when particle 17976 became entrained in a LC ring in year 33 and migrated westward (Figure 13D). Particle 17976 was still near 400-m depth when it reached in the northwestern GOM and then took four years to ascend to 100-m depth. Many particles eventually rise above 500-m depth in the south-central and southwestern portions of the GOM, but the only particles that rose above 200-m depth were entrained in LC rings in the northwestern GOM. The upward motion of particles in the northwestern GOM is thought to be associated with the spin down of LC rings. The ascent of particles into the surface layer in the northwestern GOM is repeated in the following 3 experiments and will be discussed in more detail in sections 3.2 through 3.4.

Particles that remain in the central and western portions of the deep GOM are observed to continually circulate. The 15-year paths of two particles that were initialized in the deep western basin are presented in Figure 14. Particle 1007 was initialized at 2800-m depth and primarily remained in a region that was over 3000 m deep in the southern portion of the western

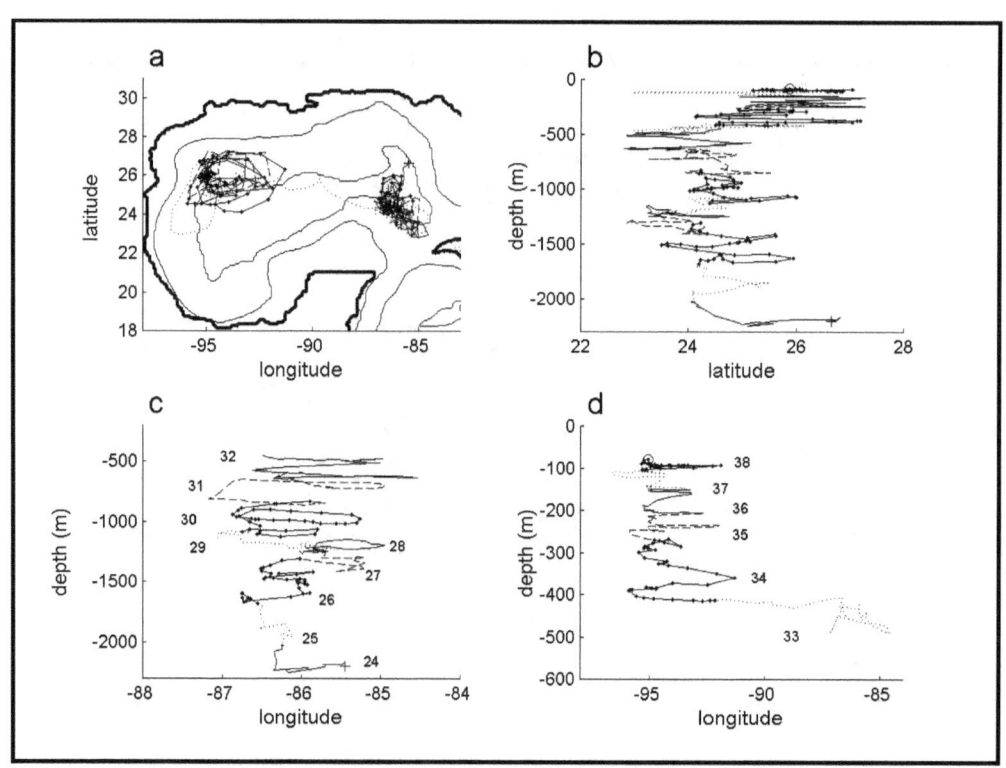

Figure 13. Path of particle 17976: (a) plan view for years 24-38, (b) latitude-depth projection for years 24-38, (c) longitude-depth projection while 17976 was in the eastern basin, (d) longitude-depth projection after 17976 became entrained in Ring S17 in year 33.

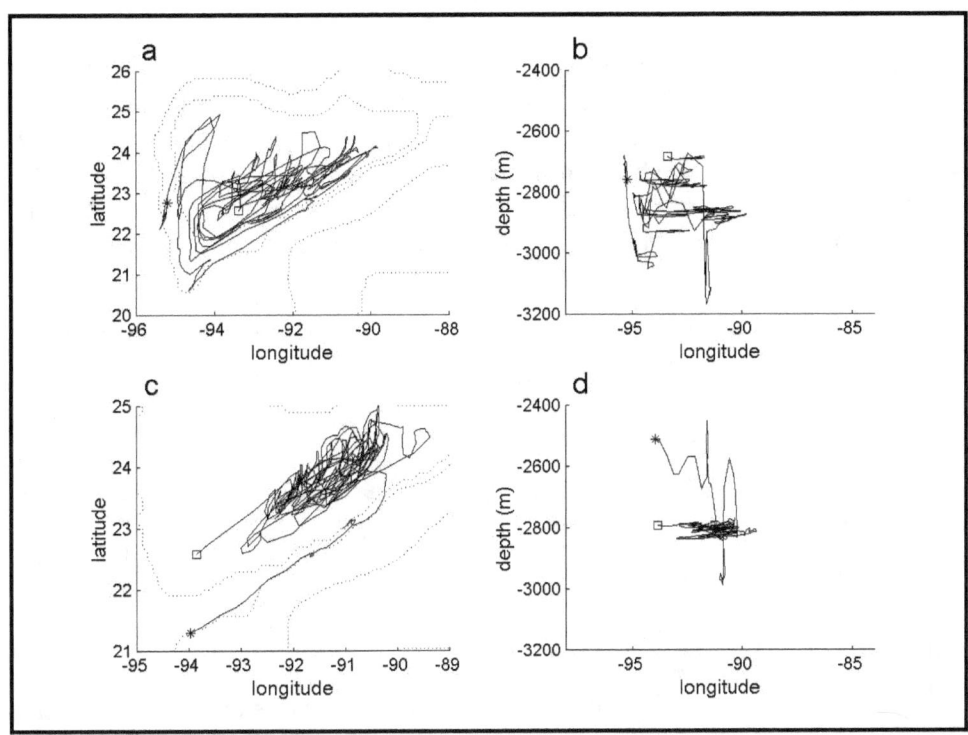

Figure 14. Paths of two particles in the deep GOM during years 24-38: (a) plan view of particle 1007, (b) longitude-depth projection of particle 1007, (c) plan view of particle 4005, and (d) longitude-depth projection of particle 4005.

basin for the entire 15 years (Figure 14 A,B). Particle 4005 was initialized at 2500 m over the western Campeche escarpment, but moved over the region that is deeper than 3000 m during the first part of year 25 and remained at almost exactly a depth of 2800 m for the next 13 years (Figure 14 C,D).

The rate at which particles ascend to 2000 m from 2200 m or below is approximately 0.34% per year from Figure 8. At this rate it would take 294 years for all particles to reach the Yucatan Channel sill depth. The rate is slightly less for particles reaching 1000 m. If the flushing of these inert particles is representative of the turnover of waters in the deep GOM, then a model residence time for deep water is at least 300 years. Figures 11 through 13 demonstrate that the loss of particles from the deep is correlated with the frequency of ring separations from the LC. The average ring separation period in this model is 6.5 months, which is smaller than the average value of 9.5 months reported for 33 observed separation intervals (Sturges and Leben 2000). The ascent of particles in the model is correlated with the separation of rings from the LC, which means the mean model separation interval is controlling the rate of flux of particles from the deep. Since the average interval of model ring separations is small, the model residence time of deep water is underestimated. If the average separation interval was longer, then the calculated rate of ascent would likely be reduced, and the model residence time would increase.

24

3.2   Experiment 2: Surface Water Tracer Particle Release

The model is initialized with 28,294 particles - one per grid box in the top two layers centered at 12.5 m and 37.5 m. The positions of these particles were tracked every 10 days for year 24 through 29 (which were repeated from Experiment 1). Approximately 20% of all particles were flushed into the North Atlantic and less than 5% were flushed into the Caribbean (Figure 15). A low percentage of particles sunk below 50 m (whether the particles started at 12.5 m or 37.5 m). The majority of particles fluctuate between the top two grid levels.

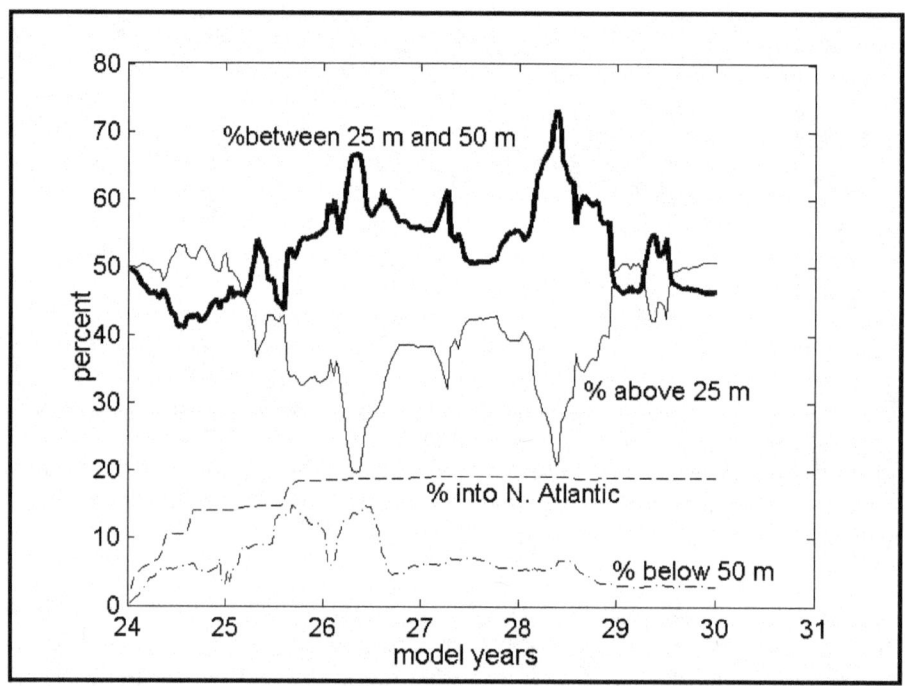

Figure 15. Percentages of particles found at specific depth ranges during Experiment 2.

Several particles that descended below 50 m were tracked to determine where they were sinking. Figures 16 and 17 show examples of two particles that descended ~70 m upon reaching the southwestern edge of the west Florida shelf during the latter part of model year 24. The descent of these particles occurred for all of model year 25 and part or all of year 26. This behavior was observed for most particles entering the region bounded by 25°N:27°N and 85°W:84°W. Some particles were stranded in this region and others moved away from the topography and became entrained in the LC. Particle 19829 became entrained in LC ring S6 at the end of year 26 and particle 7453 became entrained in LC ring S7 during year 27 and both particles migrated westward at a nearly constant depth. The descent of particles in this region did not appear to be correlated with fluctuations in the lateral area of the LC and the cause of sinking in this region was not determined. Sinking of some particles also occurs along the flanks of the entrance to the Southern Straits of Florida.

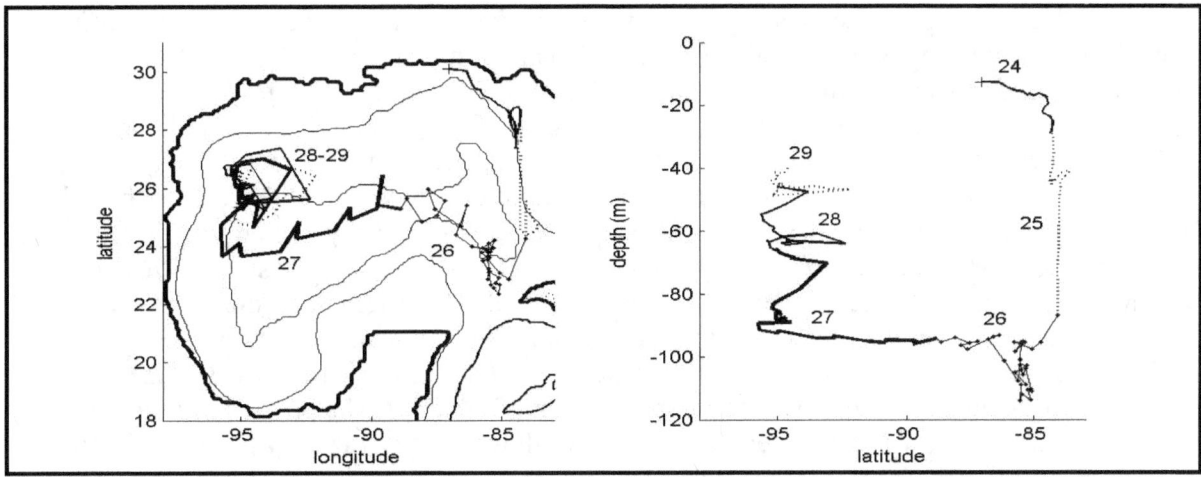

Figure 16. Path of particle 19829 path during years 24-29 in plan view and cross-sectional view.

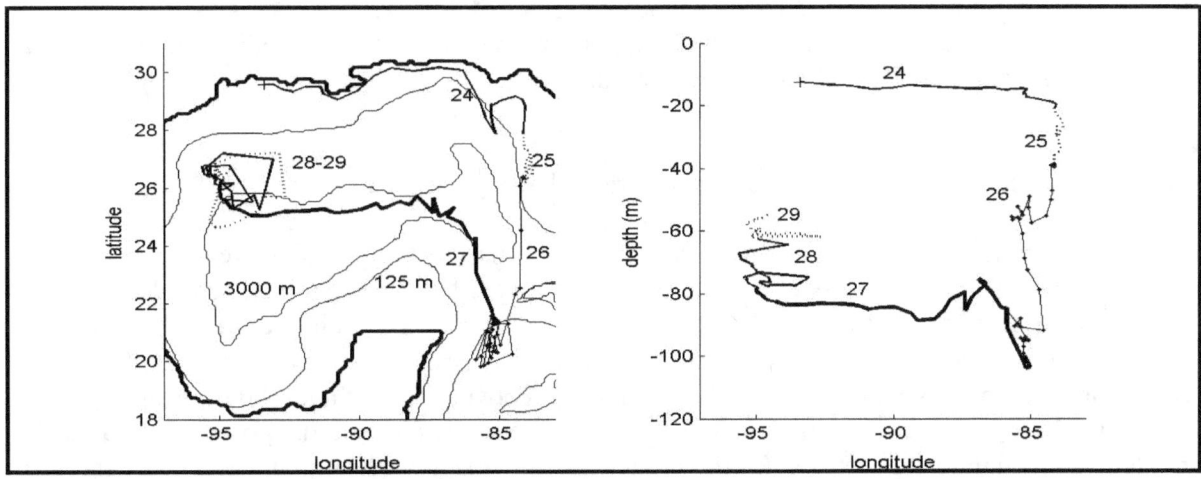

Figure 17. Path of particle 7453 path during years 24-29 in plan view and cross-sectional view.

Several particles that were initialized at 12.5 m remained in the upper 50 m during the entire 5 years. The starting location for particle 22825 was near 24.5°N and 86.5°W at 12.5 m. It crossed the GOM from ~87°W to ~95°W and back two and a half times while remaining above 40 m. The particle ascended in the western GOM and descended in the eastern GOM, but remained at nearly the same depth as it migrated through the back and forth. This particle was twice transported into the entrance to the DeSoto Canyon where it completed several anticyclonic loops before moving southward and becoming entrained in another LC ring. The particle spent the entire fifth year in the northwest corner at between 27 m and 32 m. Particles 7453 and 19829 also completed several anticyclonic spiral as they ascended in the water column in the eddy graveyard.

The physical processes associated with the spin down of warm core rings in the GOM have been examined by Schmitz and Vastano (1976) and Flierl and Mied (1985). A parametric model was used to compute diffusion and entrainment in simulated LC ring. The mean velocity field and streamline patterns were computed for a range of eddy coefficients. For the optimum case the water enters the ring at 1200 m, is transported upward, and flows outward either above 400m or below 800 m. There is a wedge-like layer between 400 m and 800 m where the velocity is directed inward. The 17° isotherm migrates upward by .8 m per day, which is equivalent to a net transport into the idealized ring of approximately 1 Sv (Schmitz and Vastano 1976). Flierl and Mied (1985) used numerical model to look at vertical radial circulation during the spin down of warm-core rings. In the case where the momentum diffusion dominates over buoyancy diffusion, there is inflow toward the center of the ring in the deep water (below 600 m), flow upward in the center, and outflow in the upper portion of the ring. The process of inflow in the lower layer and outflow in the upper layer with upwelling in the center may be applicable to the spin down of LC rings in the northwestern GOM.

The results of Experiment 2 were difficult to analyze, since a small percentage of particles remained over deep water. Many particles were either flushed-out of the GOM or drifted into shallow shelf water. Only 15% of the particles remaining in the GOM were found below 50 m, thereby making it difficult to locate regions of sinking. Another approach to locating regions of downward motion in the upper layer would be to repeatedly seed the surface layer with particles and track them for shorter duration.

3.3 Experiment 3: Base of Mixed Layer Tracer Particle Release

Experiment 3 was designed to look at the locations and processes where the particles are transported from above the mixed layer to below the mixed layer. The mixed layer depth in this model was determined from vertical profiles of temperature, salinity, and density at six equally spaced locations along 25°N. The profiles represent the average of twelve years (years 24-35) of model data for January and July. The pycnocline lies between 130 m and 180 m in summer and nearer to130 m in winter, which compares well with the climatological data used to initialize the model. This might be expected since the model was initialized with annual mean hydrographic data, but the model profiles represent 12-year seasonal means after 23 years of spin-up.

For Experiment 3 the model was seeded with 18814 particles at levels 5 and 6, centered at 128.1 m and 181.5 m, respectively. The experiment was run for 3 years of model time (years 24 through 26 were repeated). By the end of year 26, more than 60% of particles were located above 100 m, nearly 30% were located between 100 m and 200 m, and less than 10% were located below 200 m (Figure 18). Particles crossed the 200-m isobath in the ring separation region, along the ring migration paths, the Campeche Escarpment, the Texas-Louisiana slope, the DeSoto Canyon, and the entrance to the Southern Straits of Florida. Tracer particles were observed to cross the 250-m isobath in the ring separation region, Southern Straits of Florida and the Texas-Louisiana slope.

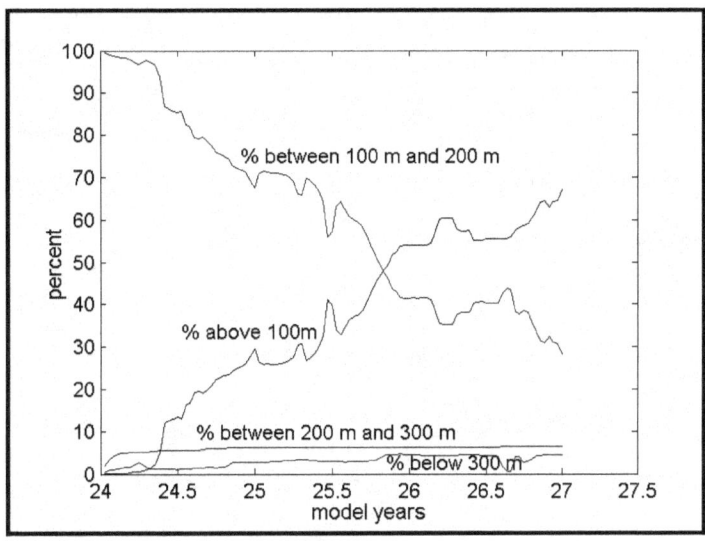

Figure 18. Percentages of particles found at specified depth ranges during Experiment 3.

The index numbers of several particles that crossed the 200-m isobath in the ring separation region were identified and the paths of these particles were tracked for the entire three years (Figure 19). All particles started in a small patch along the northeastern slope of the Yucatan Peninsula. Within the first 10 days after initialization, the entire patch of particles descended along the slope toward the north and then became entrained in LC ring S1. Except for particle 14735 (Figure 19F), the particles were located at approximately 26°N, 92°W at the end of the first year. The depth at which westward migration occurred ranged from 180 m to 270 m. After the first year the particles paths greatly diverged. The greatest ascent of particles takes place in the northwestern GOM as the particles move up over the Texas slope. The particles tend to remain at nearly the same depth as they transit the deep water away from the boundaries.

Rapid vertical motion was observed by particles 14727 (Figure 19 E) and 15049 (Figure 19C) as they encountered the upper slope off of Louisiana between 90°W and 93°W during the second half of year 25. Particle 14727 ascended from a depth of 210 m on day 200 to 160 m on day 260 at fairly even rate of upward motion. Particle 15049 first descended from 160 m on day 220 to ~200 m on day 240 and then began to ascend again on day 300 to nearly 140 m on day 350. The circulation in this region was dominated by the presence of LC ring S3 and a cyclonic eddy that formed on the eastern side of the ring (Figure 20). The particles 14727 and 15049 were adjacent to the vertical wall between levels 5 and 6 with a base of 212.5 m. Particle 14727 ascended along the northeastern margin of the cyclonic eddy and particle 15049 descended along the northeastern margin of ring S3. In Figure 20 there is an area of upwelling near 93°W, 27.7°N at the location where particle 14727 was observed to ascend. Two months later on day 300 of year 25, ring S3 and the cold-core eddy had migrated westward (Figure 21). Particle 14727 then moved eastward at a nearly constant depth, but particle 15049 was now positioned along the northern edge of the cyclonic eddy and had begun to ascend. In Figure 21 there is an area of upwelling near 90.5°W, 27.8°N on day 300 in the region where particle 15049 was ascending.

28

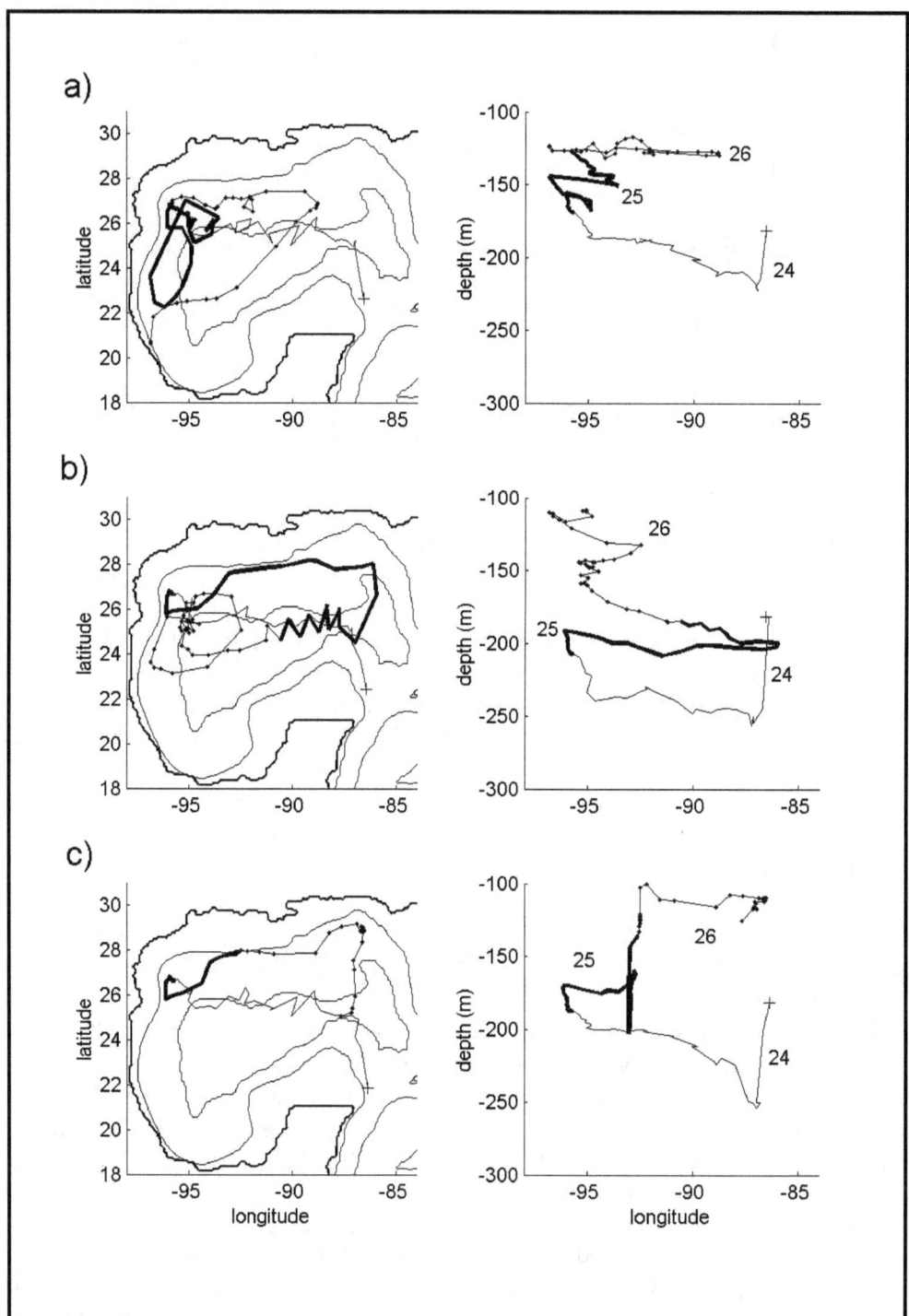

Figure 19. Plan view and longitude-depth cross-section of particles (a) 14737, (b) 14892, and (c) 15049. The year of observation is indicated.

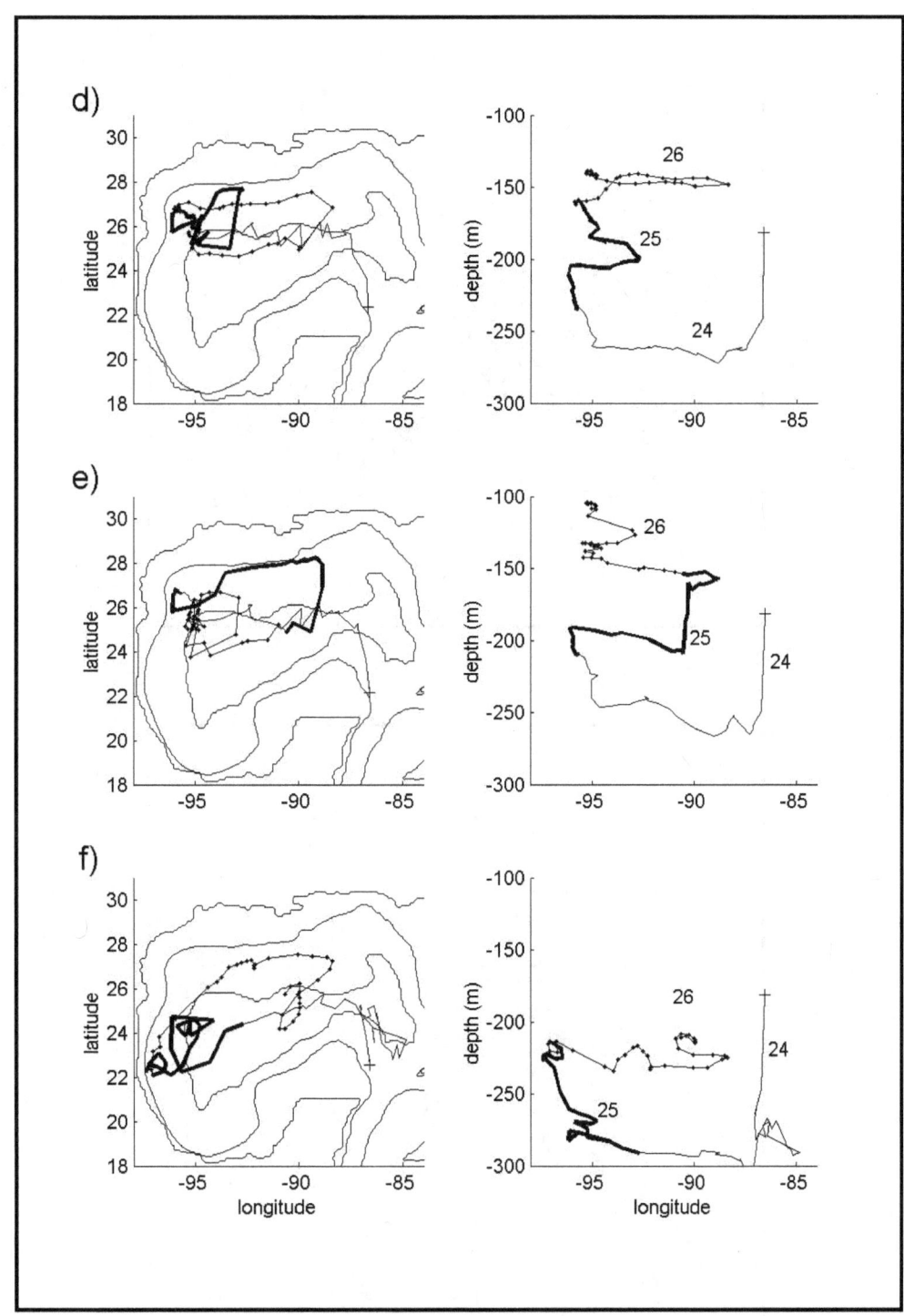

Figure 19. Plan view and longitude-depth projection of particles (d) 14579, (e) 14727, and (f) 14735. The year of observation is indicated.

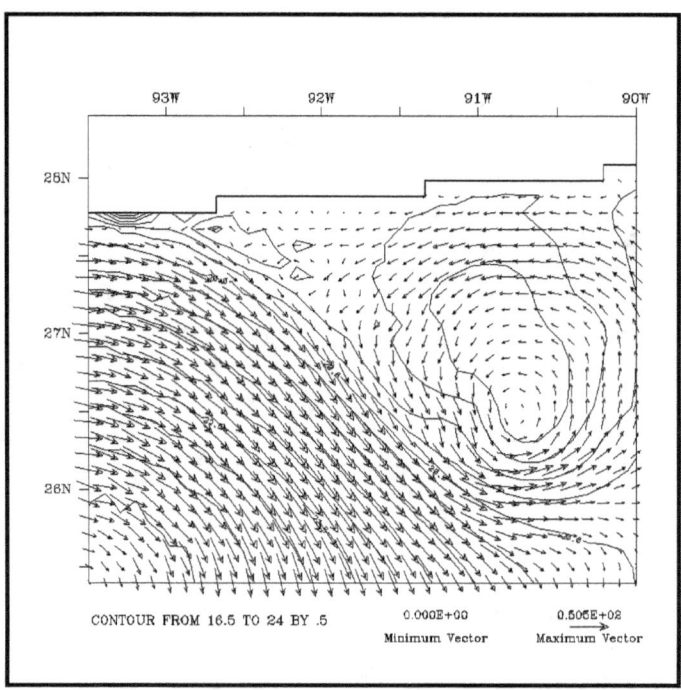

Figure 20. Velocity (cm s^{-1}) and temperature (°C) at 181.125 m on model year 25, day 240.

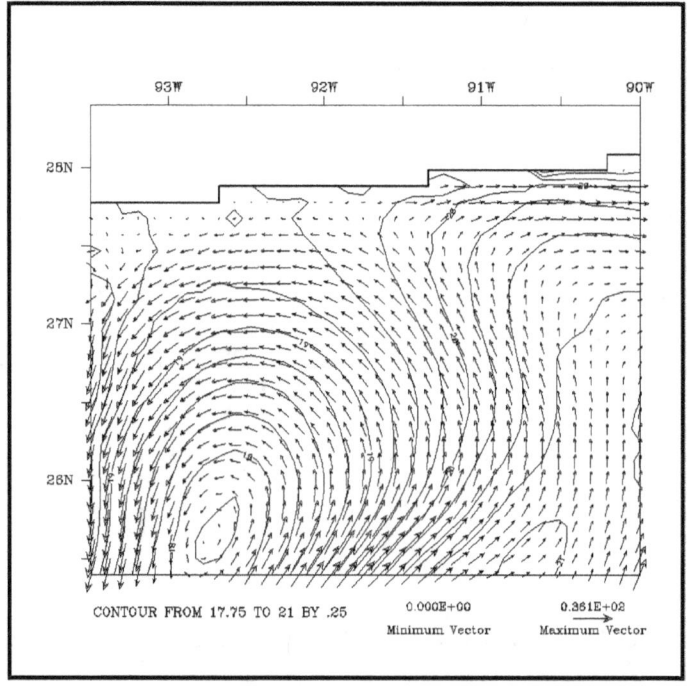

Figure 21. Velocity (cm s^{-1}) and temperature (°C) at 181.125 m on model year 25, day 300.

There are several possible explanations for the vertical motion of these particles. The fact that they did cross isopycnals during their ascent and descent suggests that the particles were moving within a bottom boundary layer, except that they were against a vertical wall. Fluid was being transported toward the wall in the vicinity of particle 14727, and the convergence of the flow at the boundary may have generated vertical velocities resulting in vertical transport. As the fluid encountered the wall, the fluid may have moved upward rather than downward because of the topography below. The opposite occurred for particle 15049, which moved down as fluid was transported away from the boundary. It is reasonable for the fluid to be drawn down from above because of the topography below.

Another explanation for the vertical displacements of particles against the wall could be that the particle tracing method is not reliable near vertical walls in the presence of strong flows. An argument against this is that the particle displacements were consistent and reasonable in terms of direction, distance displaced, and rate of movement.

3.4   Experiment 4: Level 11 (1000 m) Particle Release

From previous modeling studies and observations, 1000-m appears to be a transition depth from the LC/LC ring dominated upper layer to the vertically homogeneous lower layer. Strong mid-depth currents have been reported by SAIC, NOAA, and Texas A&M (Nowlin et al. 2001). Sporadic strong currents have been observed during offshore exploration by the oil and gas industry at slightly shallower depths. Particles released in Experiments 1 through 3 were found at 1000 m near the boundaries or in the eastern GOM. This experiment was designed to provide information about the vertical and lateral advection of particles near 1000-m depth. The simulation of model years 24 through 26 was repeated with 7594 particles initialized at the center of level 11 (1000 m). Over the three-year period, more than 70% of all particles which were initially in the east region within level 11 moved above 850 m or below 1150 m. Less than 6% descended below level 11. The remaining ~64% were found within level 10 (between 550 m and 850 m) at the end of three years. Approximately 20% of all particles that originated in the central region and 10% of all particles that originated in the west region ascended to level 10. A negligible number of particles from the west region descended below level 11 and less than 3 % of particles from the central region descended below level 11.

As in the previous three experiments, individual particles were tracked to determine where particles were moving vertically in the water column and why. The greatest vertical motion was found in the ring separation region between 85°W and 87°W at 25°N. Significant vertical motion was also observed in the northwest GOM and in the Southern Straits of Florida. Lateral motion of particles released at 1000 m was quite interesting. Particle paths in the Campeche Bay had different characteristics depending on whether they were over water depths greater than 3000 m or if they were over the slope. Particles observed over the deep, relatively flat bottom, moved in large cyclonic gyres (200 to 250 km diameters) with tight cyclonic spirals imbedded in their paths (Figure 22). Over the slope, the particle paths became elongated ellipses primarily in the southwest to northeast direction (Figure 23). Particle 4100 made repeated cyclonic loops as it migrated along the Campeche Escarpment from the southern Campeche Bay to the northern tip of Campeche Bank over a three year period. Particle 3100 oscillated back and forth over the 3-year period and was positioned southwest of its starting point after three years.

32

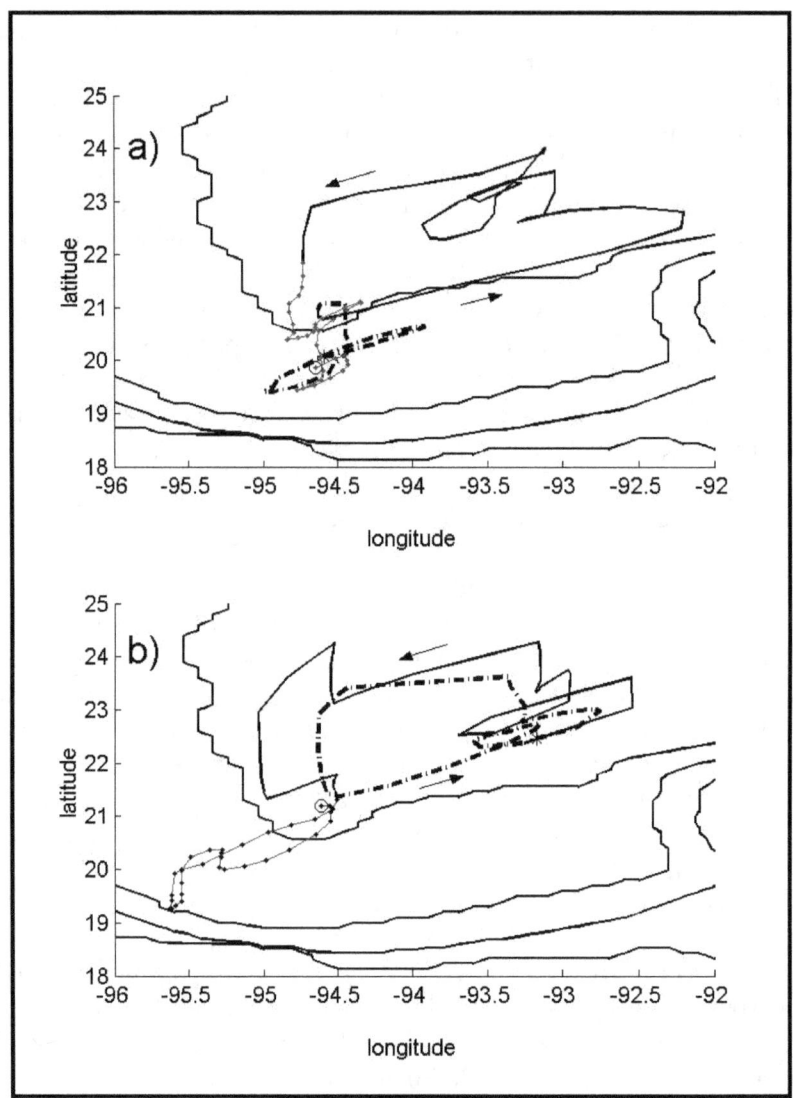

Figure 22. Particles (a) 1500 and (b) 2500 in the Campeche Bay during model years 24-26.
These particles remained at depths between 925 m and 1010 m.

An examination of particle paths over the northern slope of the GOM was also made. A
line of particles from 93.95°W to 86.45°W at 26.95°N with .5 degree spacing was tracked for 3
years. Particles west of 93°W moved immediately south and west. Two of these particles
remained in the northwest GOM, but one particle moved into the Campeche Bay and completed
several cyclonic loops similar to the paths of particles described. Particles from 89.5°W to
92.5°W moved to the northeast into the DeSoto Canyon. Particles east of 89.5°W moved
southward into the ring separation region of which 4 particles ascended to above 750 m. These
four particles made the largest vertical excursion of all the particles.

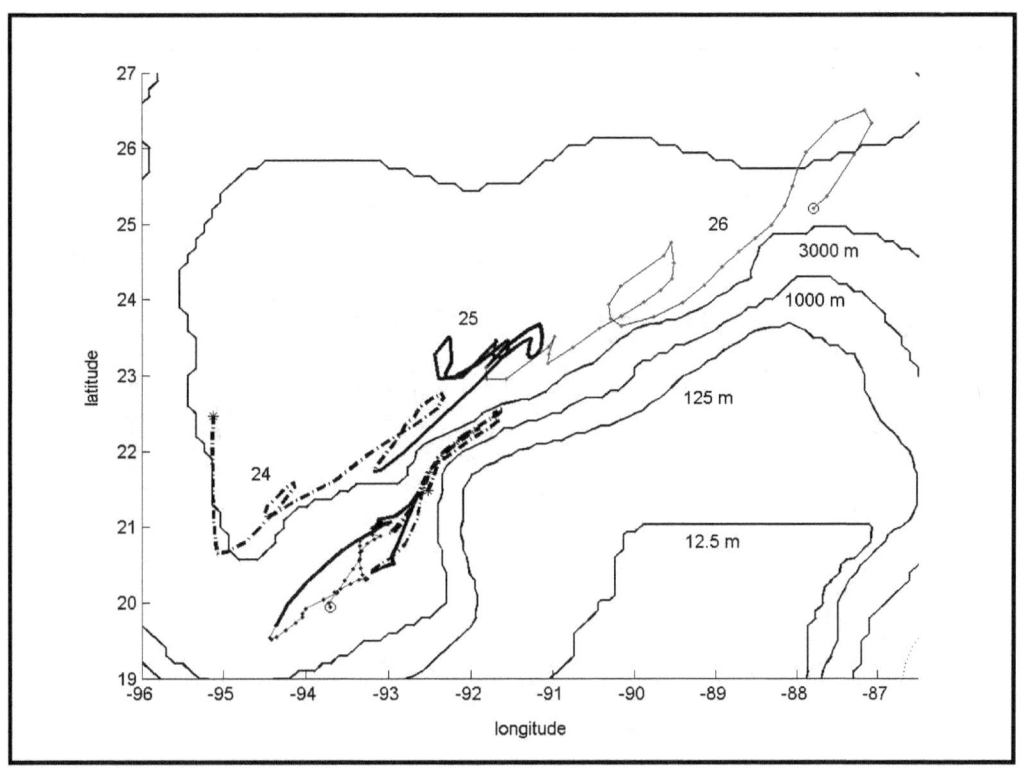

Figure 23. Particles 1100 and 3100 in the Campeche Bay during model years 24-26. These particles were initialized at 1000 m.

3.5   Experiment 5: Eulerian Framework Study at 2200 m

During the first four experiments the inert particles were tracked as they moved freely about the domain. This method of tracking particles was not suitable for examining the changes in the circulation at fixed locations over time. This experiment was designed to observe the range of particle displacements over time by repeatedly seeding the same locations with particles at a fixed interval in time. 116 locations were chosen directly over the slope at a depth of 2200 m in water of depths less than or equal to 2800 m. Particles were released at the beginning of each month at each of the 116 locations and tracked every 10 days for 30 days over a two-year period.

The particle motion is primarily along slope around the entire basin (Figure 24). Topographic rectification is apparent along the 2200-m isobath from 87°W to 95°W along the northern slope and again from 88°W to 95°W along the southern slope. The maximum lateral displacements observed along the western slope over the 30-day sequences are nearly 2 degrees of latitude (~200 km), which is equivalent to sustained speeds of nearly 8 cm s^{-1}. The maximum straight-line lateral displacements over a 30-day period in the north central GOM and the south central GOM are approximately 100 km and 150 km, respectively. The maximum rate of displacement by particles in these regions was 4 to 6 cm s^{-1} over 30 days.

34

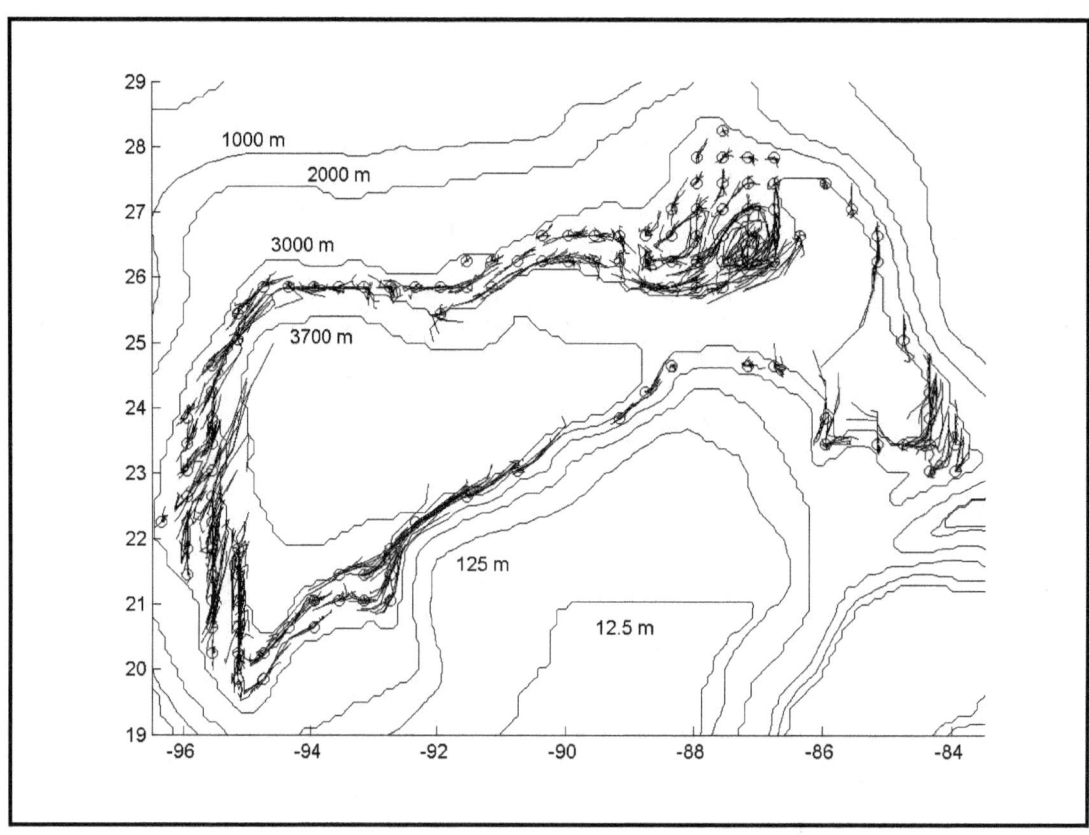

Figure 24. 30-day particle displacements for each month in model year 25.

The method of repeatedly initializing the particles at a given location every 30 days was very useful for examining the vertical displacements of particles near the 2000-m isobath. Along-slope 30-day particle displacements versus depth are plotted for each of three regions in Figure 25. The vertical displacements appear large compared to the lateral displacements, but the range on the vertical axis is only 800 m, compared to more than a range of 120 km on the x-axis. The largest vertical displacements are in the entrance to the South Florida Straits near 84°W and just below the sill of the Yucatan Channel (Figure 25A). The vertical displacements along the western slope between 22°N and 25°N are generally less than ~200m. In the latitude band between 25°N and 28°N, there is a cluster of larger than average vertical displacement vectors near 92W where the Sigsbee Escarpment protrudes southward (Figure 25B) and again at 95°W. The average 30-day vertical displacement vectors along the northern slope are less than ~100m. Along the western slope (west of 94.5°W) (Figure 25C), the average vertical displacement is the smallest of the three regions (except for the northwest corner). The particle trajectories along the western slope south of 25°N exhibit a greater cross-slope component in the x-y projection. Particle displacements may be affected in this region by LC rings and deep eddies are colliding with the western slope.

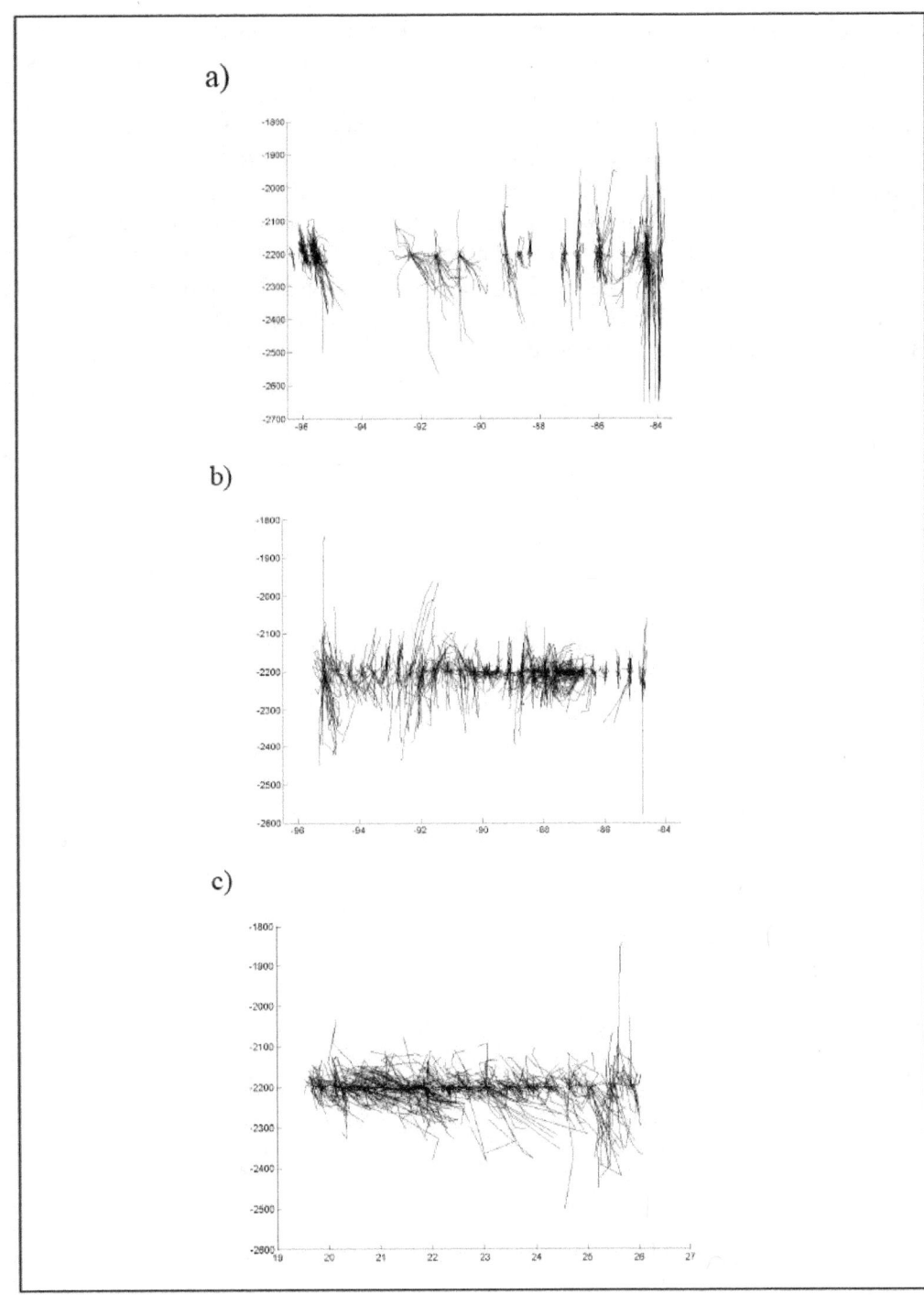

Figure 25. Vertical displacements of particles during model years 24 and 25 of Experiment 5:
(a) all particles between 22°N and 25°N, (b) all particles between 25°N and 28°N,
and (c) all particles west of 94.5°W.

Particle displacements are oriented along slope and appear to oscillate back and forth. The time dependence of these oscillations was examined by plotting the 30-day along-slope component versus time for several particles in different locations (Figure 26). There is a strong correlation between the times each current switched direction and the shedding of a LC ring. In the far eastern GOM at 84.35W, 23.45N the current switched from east to west immediately following the separation of rings S1 through S4 (Figure 26A). At the base of the Mississippi Fan (-87.95W, 26.25N) there is a shift from westward currents to eastward current coinciding with the separation of rings S1 through S3 (Fig 26B). There is some variability in the timing of these events due to the variability of the ring size and proximity of the rings to the bathymetry. Over the Sigsbee Escarpment at 91.15W, 25.85N the currents flow toward the west at the time of ring separation and switch to the east between shedding events (Fig. 26C).

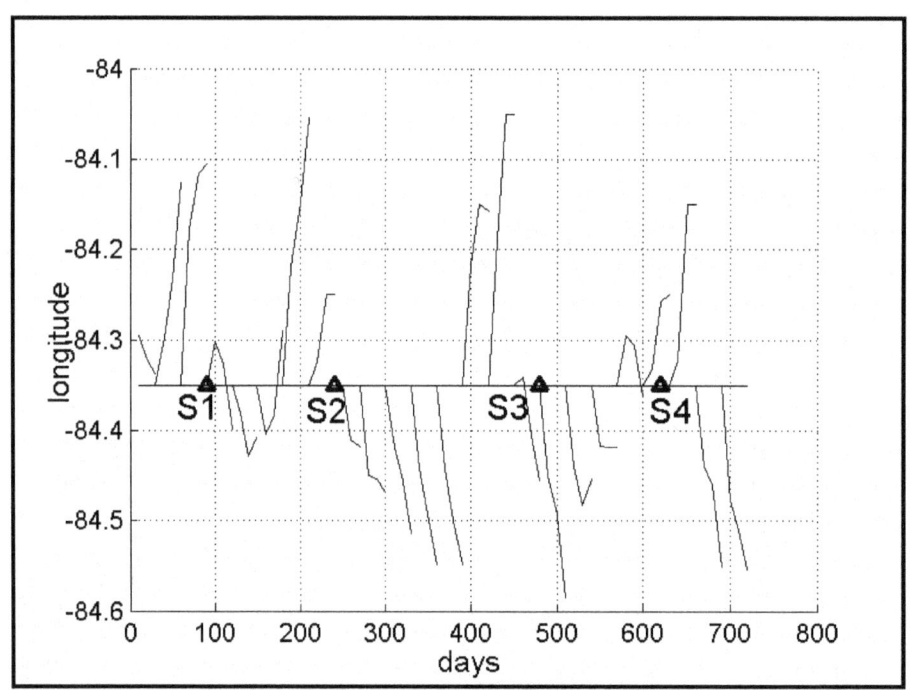

Figure 26A. 30-day longitude displacement vectors for particle 112 at 84.35°W, 23.45°N.

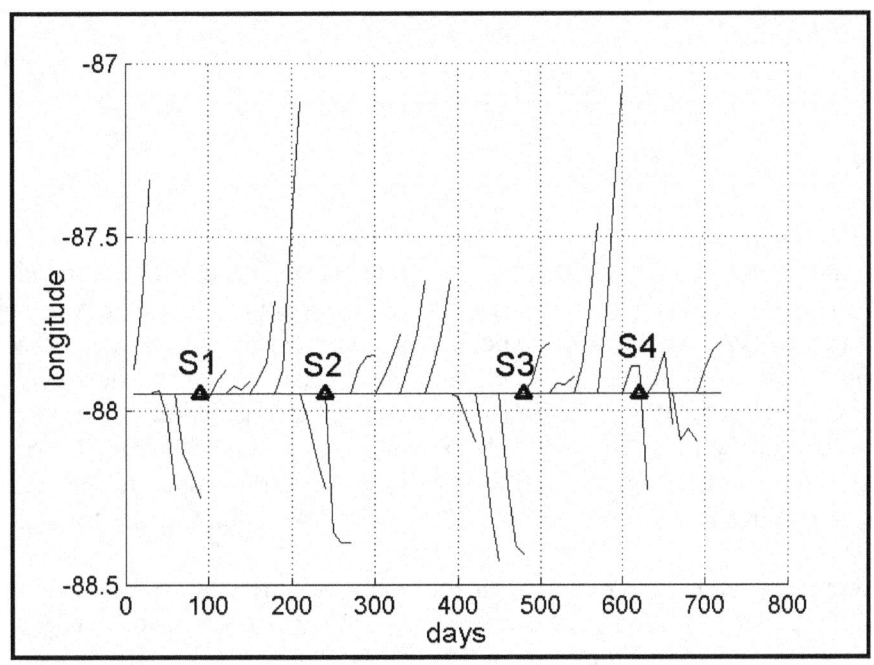

Figure 26B. 30-day longitude displacement vectors for particle 77 at 87.95°W, 26.25°N.

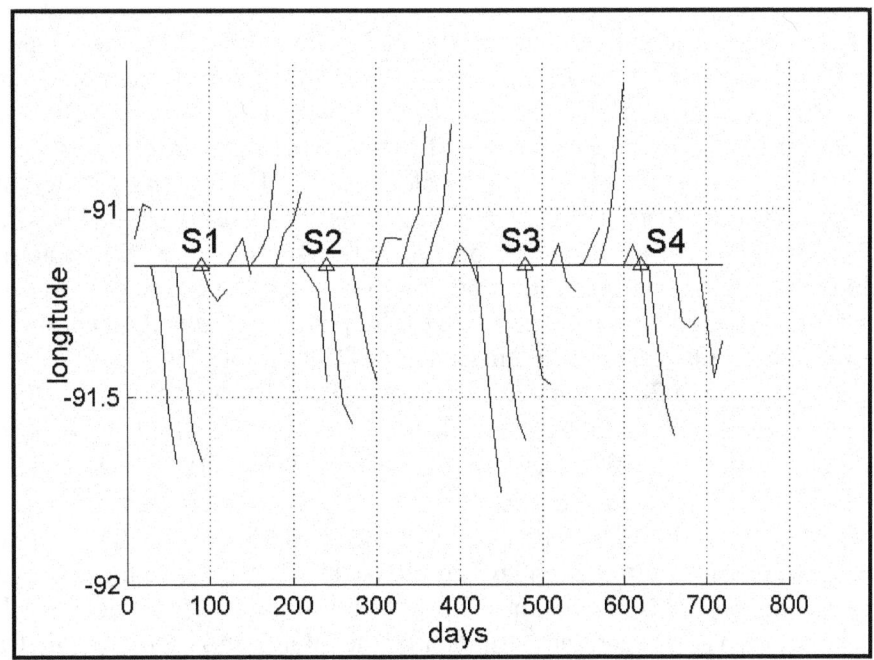

Figure 26C. 30-day longitude displacement vectors for particle 54 at 91.15°W, 25.85°N

CHAPTER 4

MEAN CIRCULATION

4.1   Deep Mean Hydrographic and Velocity Fields

One of the main objectives of this project has been to look at ventilation of the deep water. The area beneath the LC was identified as an important region for the upward flux of particles from the deep waters. Downward flux appears to occurring primarily along the boundaries. Water mass distribution in the deep was examined by plotting the 12-year average hydrographic and flow fields at various levels (Figure 27). In the near-surface level the LC extends northwestward into the central GOM transporting relatively warm, saline water (Figure 27A). Upwelling at the Catoche Tongue of the Yucatan Peninsula greatly influences the hydrography of the entire Campeche Bank. The eddy graveyard is apparent in the mean as an anticyclone in the northwestern corner of the GOM. A weak cyclone is observed in the western half of the Campeche Bay

At 1000 m depth the most noticeable features in the temperature field is the upwelling of relatively cool, fresh water around the eastern side of the Yucatan Peninsula (Figure 27B) which extends westward from the tip of the Yucatan Peninsula. An area of relatively warm water is observed in the northwest GOM from 1000 m to 1600 m (Figure 27B). There is a depression of the isotherms in this region due to the anticyclonic circulation of the decaying LC rings. This region is also an active area for vertical motion of tracer particles as evidenced in Experiments 1 through 4.

A band of relatively cool water is observed along the slope off the southwest coast of Florida at every level down to 3100 m. From 1600 m to 1900 m cool water appears to enter through the Yucatan Channel along the northwestern tip of Cuba. The relatively cool water is then advected northward along the eastern side of the mean cyclonic circulation. An anticyclone is positioned just to the northwest of the mean cyclonic flow. This mean cyclone-anticyclone pair is highly coherent in the vertical from 1600 m to 3100 m and is contained by the 3000-m contour. Relatively cool water also appears to be advected southward by the eastern side of the mean anticyclone and is possibly being upwelled by the interaction of the current with the slope. The coldest water is observed on the eastern side of the juncture of the cyclone-anticyclone and is advected toward the southwest between the centers of the cyclone-anticyclone pair.

From 2200 m through 2800 m mean cyclonic flow is observed along the 3000-m contour in the western and central basins to the west of 86°W. This mean cyclonic flow is concentrated at or very near the boundary at 3100 m and 3400 m. The temperature gradients in the deep are extremely small (.017°C at 3100 m and .005°C at 3400 m), but the temperature patterns are repeated from 2500 m to the bottom. The isotherms tilt up to the north in the central Gulf, which is consistent with the cyclonic circulation around the basin. These modeling observations are consistent with the theory that North Atlantic Deep Water overflows the Yucatan Sill on the east side, flows counterclockwise around the perimeter of the GOM, and returns to the Caribbean through the west side of the Yucatan Channel (Maul et al. 1985).

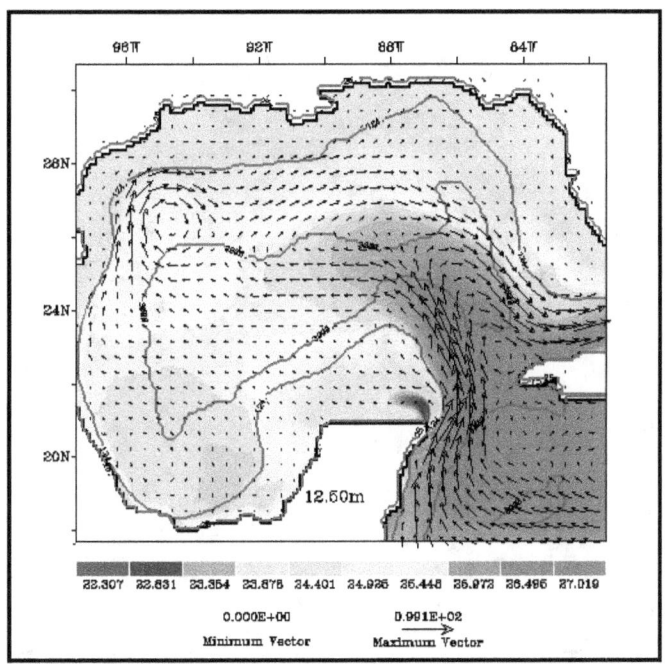

Figure 27A. 12-year average model temperature (°C) and velocity vectors (cm s⁻¹) at 12.5 m.

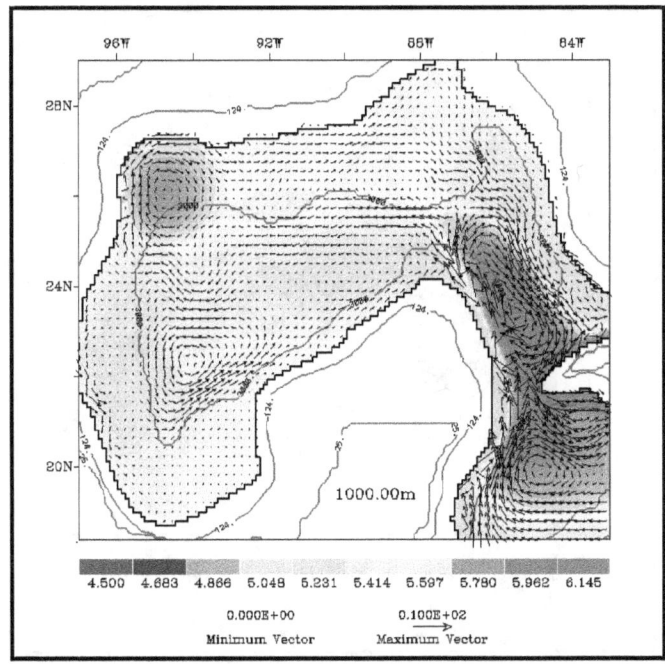

Figure 27B. 12-year average model temperature (°C) and velocity vectors (cm s⁻¹) at 1000 m.

40

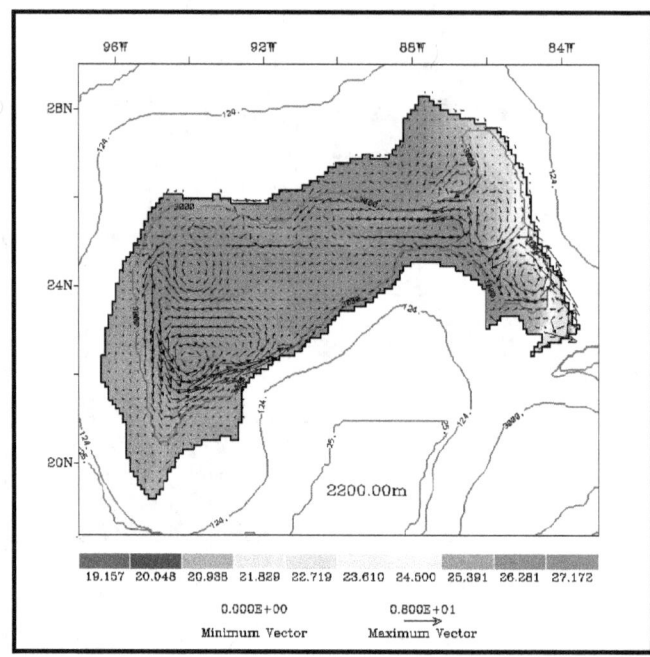

Figure 27C. 12-year average model temperature ((T-4)*100ºC) and velocity vectors (cm s^{-1}) at 2200 m.

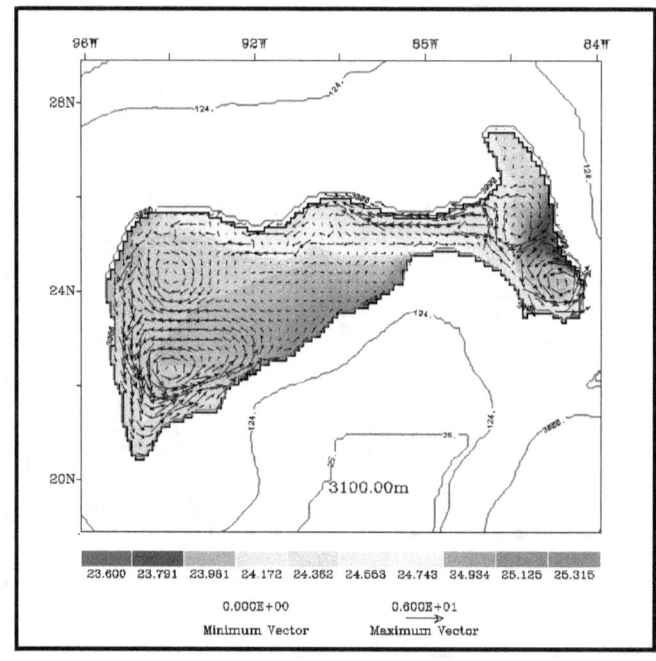

Figure 27D. 12-year average model temperature ((T-4)*100ºC) and velocity vectors (cm s^{-1}) at 3100 m.

The mean cyclonic circulation around the deep basin below 2000m is in good agreement with University of Colorado Princeton Ocean Model (CUPOM) output for years 1993 through 1999 (Nowlin et al. 2001). Another similarity between these models is the anticyclonic current flowing along the 1000 m contour off the Mexico slope at 24N to the Louisiana slope near 90W. An important feature of both models is the deep mean cyclonic gyre centered at approximately 24.5N and 85W, which has a companion anticyclonic gyre positioned just northwest of the cyclone. There are differences in the mean surface circulation between this model and CUPOM. The mean position of the LC is similar, although the LC extends farther west in the this model resulting in a mean westward current in the center of the GOM and an eastward current south of Louisiana between 26N and 28N. The CUPOM model circulation features an anticyclone centered over the axis of the DeSoto Canyon at 88W, 29N whereas this model produces mean flow up the axis of the DeSoto Canyon. Other differences include a mean anticyclonic gyre in the CUPOM model centered at ~23.5N over the Mexican Slope, a mean cyclonic gyre in the south-western Campeche Bay in this model, and a larger anticyclonic gyre in the 'eddy graveyard' in this model, that is much weaker in the CUPOM model. Many of the differences in the surface features may be due to the surface fluxes of heat, salt, and momentum. The CUPOM model is a data assimilation model that was used to hindcast currents in the GOM from observations. This project used climatological mean fields to force the model in an effort to reproduce the LC system, as well as the prevailing seasonal circulation features.

4.2   Kinetic Energy Distribution

By initializing the model with particles at 2200 m and recording their 30-day displacements, particle motion was observed to be primarily along the slope. This was especially true in the central and western basin of the GOM. The deep mean flow fields described in the preceding section suggest that there is cyclonic flow around the perimeter of the deep central and western portions of the GOM. Significant advection of particles could result from energetic events and wave phenomena. Recent efforts to model deep water in the GOM, including several projects funded by Minerals Management Service, primarily focus on energy levels associated with Topographic Rossby Waves (TRW) and jets. From the viewpoint of operational end environmental problems in the deep water, advection resulting from energetic events and wave phenomena is one of the primary issues. Therefore, in addition to examining particle advection, the kinetic energy levels in the deep are examined for evidence of wave phenomena.

The velocity at each grid point in the lower levels was saved every three days for three years during Experiment 5. The eddy kinetic energy averaged over three years was vertically coherent from 2500 m through 3100 m, with slight bottom intensification in the regions of highest eddy kinetic energy. The bands of eddy kinetic energy are within the LC ring formation region, offshore of the DeSoto Canyon, and along the slope in the central and western portions (Figure 28).

42

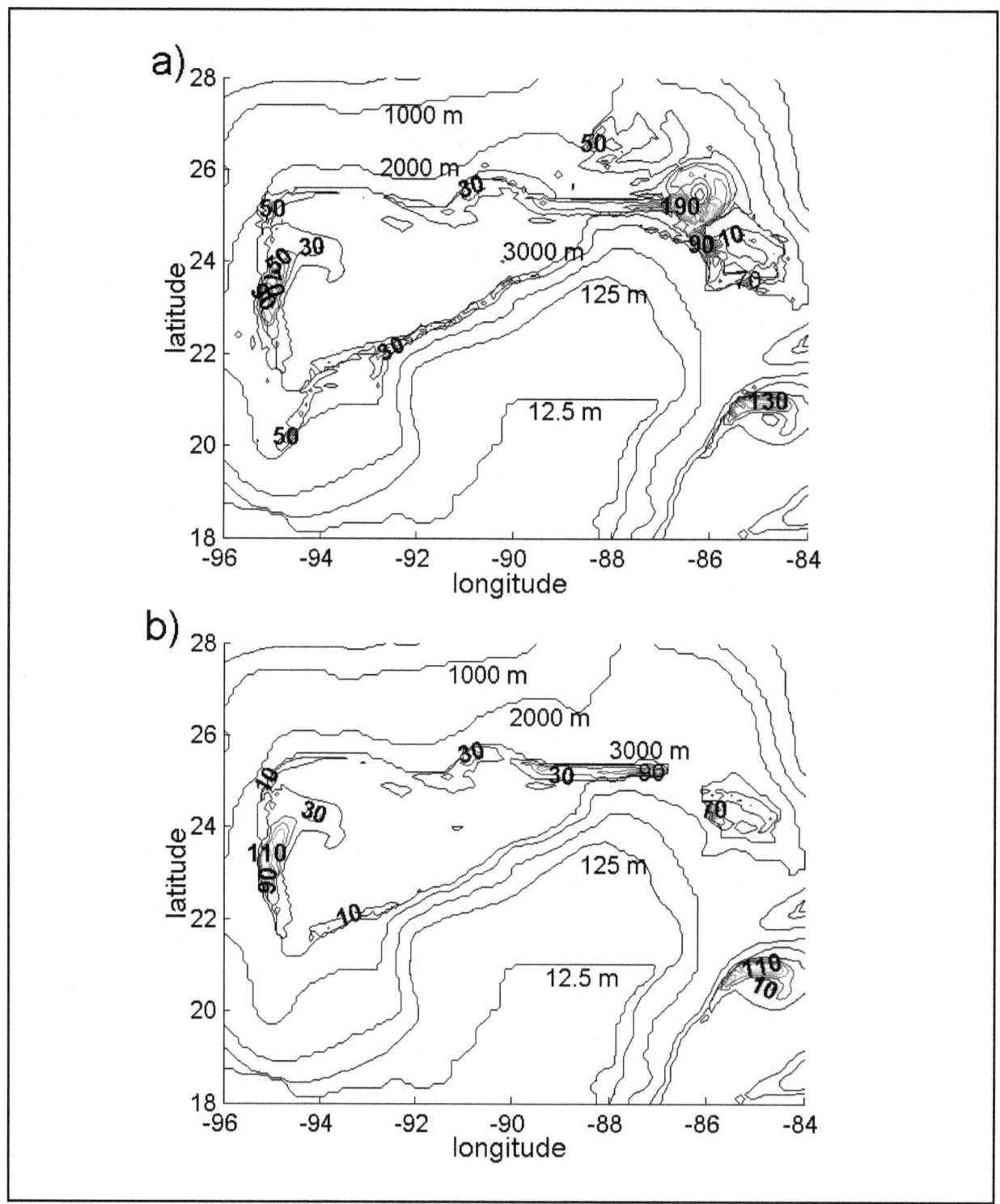

Figure 28. The 3-year average eddy kinetic energy at a) 2500 m and b) 3400 m.

The velocity data was low pass filtered with a cutoff of 180 days to look at the kinetic energy associated with the low frequency events, such as eddy shedding. The average kinetic energy computed using the low-pass filtered data is highest in the ring separation region and has smaller maxima along a band from 23°N to 25°N along the western slope (Figure 29). The original velocity data was also band pass filtered between 40 days and 10 days and used to compute the kinetic energy averaged over the three-year period. The band-passed data has several localized maxima (Figure 30). The maxima near 88°W, 92°W, and 95°W may be associated with generation regions of TRW=s.

Values for the mean kinetic energy were compared for the bottom three grid levels at seven one-degree intervals of longitude along 25.5°N. Bottom intensification of the mean kinetic energy computed from the high-pass filtered velocity fields was observed at all seven locations. The kinetic energy computed using the low-pass filtered velocity fields was analyzed for the bottom levels at the same geographic locations. The kinetic energy exhibited a slight increase toward the bottom for the low-pass filtered velocities at only 95°W, 92°W, 91°W and 89°W, but not at 94°W, 93°W, and 90°W. The bottom intensification of the high-pass filtered velocity field along the northern slope is consistent with the propagation of TRW's.

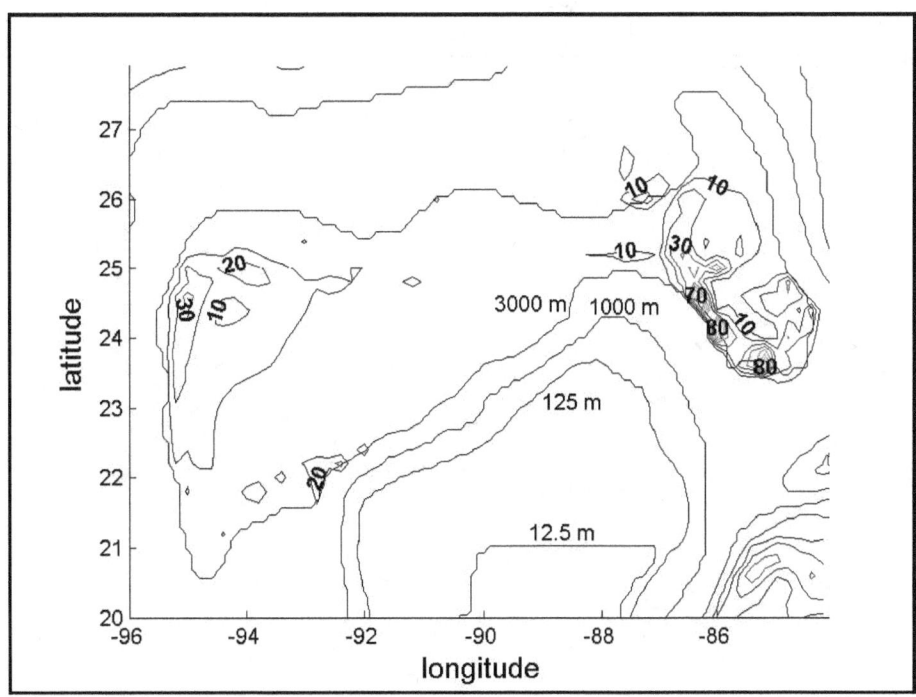

Figure 29. Low-pass filtered (180 day cut-off) kinetic energy at 2800 m averaged over 3 years.

44

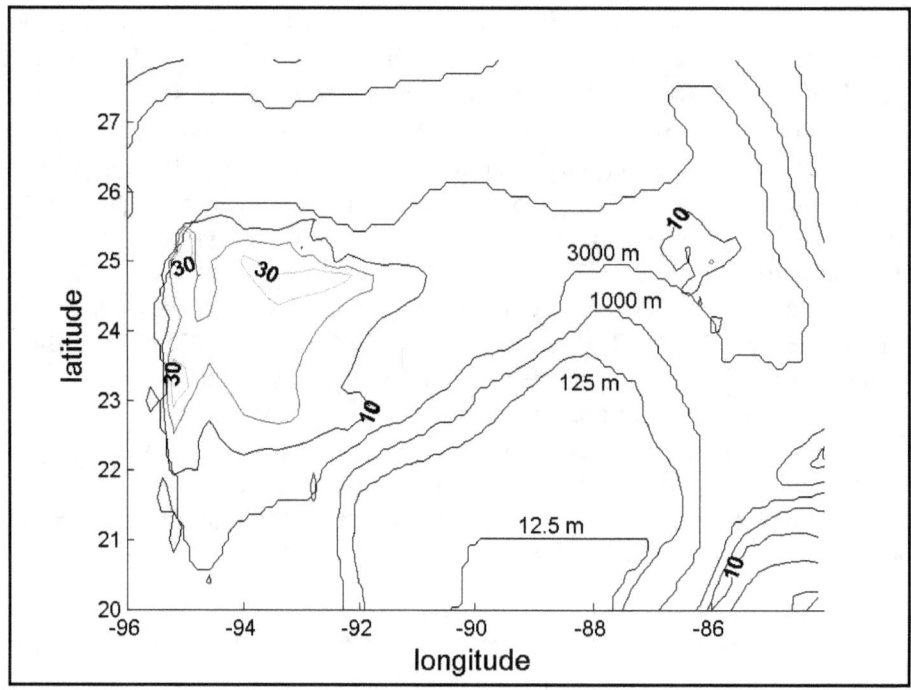

Figure 30. Band-pass filtered (40 to 10 days) kinetic energy at 2800 m
averaged over 3 years.

CHAPTER 5

DISCUSSION AND SUMMARY

5.1   Particle Paths in the Deep Water

The model was seeded below 2000 m with 19,105 inert particles that drift freely within the model domain in response to the velocity field. By tracking individual particles, it can be seen that the upward motion of particles from below 2000 m to above 1000 m occurs almost exclusively in the ring separation region in the eastern GOM. Individual particles are observed to spiral upward with each separation of a new ring from the LC. An anticyclone-cyclone eddy pair develops in the deep eastern basin each time the LC reaches its northernmost extent and sheds a ring. The tracer particles are advected away from the Campeche Bank into the deep water of the eastern basin by the northward currents on the western side of the leading anticyclone. A southward current associated with the western side of the trailing cyclonic eddy moves the particles back toward the Campeche Bank. The particles remain at nearly the same depth as they are advected away from the slope, but they move slightly upward in the water column as they are pushed back toward the slope. With each separation of a LC ring, the particles experience a net upward motion.

The deep eddy pairs, or modons, that are generated in the deep eastern basin propagate westward. There is a constriction in the bottom topography between 86.5°W and 88.5° that forms an east-west channel below 3000 m. Since the deep barotropic motions 'feel' the bottom, the eddy pairs become compressed in the north-south direction and squeeze through the channel. The eddy pairs reform on the western side of the channel and continue to propagate westward. Individual deep eddies can sometimes be tracked all the way to the western slope, and other times they become indistinguishable from the background eddy field. Although the particles in the deep are continually moved about in response to the deep eddy field, the velocities are weak compared to the upper layer eddies (<20 cm/s) and the deep eddies only transport the tracer particles short distances. During a 15-year simulation in which the waters below 2200 m were seeded with nearly 20,000 particles, fewer than 10% of particles were transported across 88°W in either direction. The advective properties of deep eddies may change as they squeeze through the deep channel, which would limit the exchange of fluid from the eastern and central basins. 17 Profile Autonomous Lagrangian Circulation Explorer (PALACE) floats were deployed in the northern GOM that were designed to drift at approximately 900 m. The floats were designed to remain at a nearly constant depth for 6.23 days and then come to the surface for 11.5 hours to transmit their geographic position to polar orbiting satellites. Weatherly (personal communication 2000) analyzed the trajectories of these floats and noted that there was limited exchange of the floats across 89°W at 900 m.

There are complex bottom topographic features over the slope that range in magnitude from carbonate mounds and salt domes (tens of meters) to submarine canyons (several kilometers). The presence of rough bottom topography implies possible topographically-induced current instability and enhanced vertical mixing (e.g., Polzin et al. 1997). To the west of the Mississippi Delta in water depths of approximately 3000 m a field of sedimentary furrows have been observed by Bryant at Texas A&M. These long, narrow channels which are oriented parallel to the escarpment and cover ~100 km may be attributed to strong near bottom flows.

During a recent current meter deployment near a depth of 2000 m the northern GOM occasional strong flows of 85 cm s^{-1} were measured (Hamilton and Lugo-Fernandez 2001). These current measurements were recorded only 10 m from the bottom while the LC was shedding an eddy. Hamilton and Lugo-Fernandez (2001) conclude that the LC and LC frontal eddies are forcing the deep layer in such a way as to generate TRW's that propagate westward with periods of 10-14 days. This study also provided evidence that near bottom currents of 40-50 cm×s^{-1} are occurring at a regular rate as wave trains continually pass over the site. A numerical study of TRW propagation in the northern GOM by Oey and Hamilton (2000) indicated that there is a concentration of kinetic energy in the 20 to 100 day band along the 3000-m isobath extending westward from under the LC.

The numerical model was seeded with particles close to the bathymetry at 2200 m. Particle positions were saved every 10 days for 30 days over a 2-year period with the particles at the same location at the beginning of every month. The particle motion near the slope exhibited topographic rectification and individual particles were transported as far as 50 km in 30 days. The direction of particle motion along the northern slope is highly correlated with the proximity of the LC and the passage of LC eddies. The vertical excursion of the particles over each 30-day interval was generally less than 20 m, but on one occasion did exceed 100 m. Since the sampling interval is10 days the particle tracers could not be used to detect TRW activity in the 10-14 day range.

Daily snapshots of model velocity fields were saved at all levels from 2200 m to 3700 m during a three-year simulation in order to compute kinetic energy in the deep water. There is relatively high concentration of eddy kinetic energy in bands along the slope below 2200 m in the model output. Slight bottom intensification of the kinetic energy in these bands in consistent with TRW propagation. The analyses of the model currents, hydrographic fields, and tracer particles strongly indicate that the deep currents are coupled with overlying upper layer features in the eastern GOM.

5.2   Particle Paths in the Upper Layer

Many particles eventually rise above 500-m depth in the south-central and southwestern portions of the GOM, but the only particles that rise above 200-m depth are entrained in LC rings in the northwestern GOM. The upward motion of particles in the northwestern GOM is thought to be associated with the shoaling of isotherms during the spin down of LC rings. The ascent of particles into the surface layer in the northwestern GOM was examined in more detail by initializing the center of each grid box in the top two grid levels with 28,294 particles and tracking their positions for 5 years.

The ultimate goal of Experiment 2 was to see if particles that were initially near the surface (above 50 m) would descend into the lower layer below 1000 m. Less than 20% of all particles were observed below 50 m at any time. The majority of particles fluctuated between the top two grid levels. Several particles that descended below 50 m were tracked to determine where they were sinking and what processes could be responsible. Particles that descended below 100 m were near the LC or LC rings. The few exceptions were in the southern Campeche Bay, the edge of the west Florida shelf, the northwestern coast of Cuba, and the Yucatan

Channel. Of the 28,294 particles, only 4 descended below 150 m during the 5-year simulation. One of these particles was located on the outer west Florida shelf near 84°W between 25°N and 27°N and the other three were on the northwest tip of Cuba. All particles that moved onto the outer west Florida shelf between 25°N and 27°N were observed to slowly descend from above 20 m to nearly 80 m over periods of up to two years. This slow descent takes place over several ring separation cycles and is not related to a single energetic event. Particles that entered the eddy graveyard typically moved upward in the water column as they completed several anticyclonic spirals, although many became entrained in the current that extends eastward along the Louisiana shelf break.

Segregation between the eastern and western basins of the GOM was observed in the behavior of 12,542 surface drifters that were released from 1955-1987 (Lugo-Fernández et al. 2001). Drifters that were recovered along the coast in the eastern GOM originated in the eastern GOM, but drifters that were recovered along the coast in the western GOM may have originated in either the eastern or western GOM. Lugo-Fernández et al. (2001) attribute this distribution of landings to prevailing easterly winds. The results from the second model experiment featuring the initialization of particle tracers in the upper 50 m of the water column are in good agreement with these observations. The following similarities are noted between the model particle tracers and the surface drifters: a general movement of particles from east to west; westward movement of particles along the outer shelf off of Louisiana during winter; and avoidance by particles of the west Florida Shelf. Eastward transport of particles in the upper layer during the first 60 days of the model simulation occurs near the coast of the northern GOM and along the northern edge of the LC. The transport of model tracer particles from the eastern basin to the central and western basins occurs primarily due to westward migration of eddies. At the end of 60 days, none of the model tracer particles that originated west of 92°W had moved to the east of 91°W, while particles initially to the east of 88°W were transported into the central GOM within a LC ring or were advected westward by the upwelling plume over the Campeche Bank.

Experiment 3 featured the initialization of particles at depths of 128 m and 181 m and provided interesting results on the behavior of particles over the outer shelf and upper slope. Vertical motion over steep topography was observed in response to strong flows. A patch of particles was observed to descend from ~181m to ~240 m during the first 10 days of model year 24 at approximately 87°W, 23°N when the LC was flowing directly over this location with current speeds greater than 1 m/s. The vertical motion of tracer particles over the upper Louisiana slope coincided with the passage of a cold-core eddy and a LC ring that produced strong currents up against the slope.

5.3   Mixing and Ventilation of the Deep Water

The deep waters of the GOM are well oxygenated (> 5.4 ml/l) with the highest near-bottom values measured in the eastern GOM and the lowest values in the far western GOM. (Berbian and Cantillo 1999). The residence time of deep water GOM is estimated to be only 100 years from both simple volume flux calculations and analysis of barium concentrations in the deep sea (Buerkert 1997). Since deep water below the sill depth is completely isolated from outside, the only mechanism to ventilate the deep water must be via vertical mixing. The results from Experiment 2 indicate that there is very little downward mixing of the surface waters. Less than 10% of all particles initially at a depth of 12.5 m descended below 50 m and only 4 particles out of more than 28,000 that were initially above 50 m descended below 150 m during a 6 year simulation (Figure 15). The results of Experiment 2 were influenced by the fact that many particles were flushed out of the GOM or became stranded near the coast.

The final experiment was designed to observe the particle tracer behavior near 2000 m over the slope and has provided the best indication of how oxygen-rich water is reaching the deep GOM. Upper North Atlantic Deep Water (UNADW) is an oxygen-rich water mass (>6. ml/l) that flows into the Cayman Basin of the Caribbean Sea over the Windward Passage (sill depth 1688 m) (Wust, 1964). UNADW then mixes with Caribbean water and flows into the Yucatan Basin. Maul et al. (1985) consider the possibility that UNADW flows into the GOM on the eastern side of the Yucatan Channel to explain the difference between T-S properties at sill depth in the Florida Straits and Yucatan Channel. Since the water in the Caribbean below the sill depth of the Yucatan Channel is cooler than water at the same depths in the GOM, it is natural to expect that the water flowing over the Yucatan sill would sink below sill depths. The largest vertical particle displacements occurred in the eastern GOM in Experiment 5. The greatest descent was observed to occur in over the steep topography north of the Yucatan Channel and west of the Southern Straits of Florida.

From the 12-year mean temperature and salinity fields, it appears that relatively cold, salty water flowing over the sill of the Yucatan Channel, hugs the eastern side of the channel and then flows northward along the eastern side of the basin. The cold water continues to follow the bathymetry and flow northward and then westward at progressively greater depths. Relatively warm water appears to upwell over the northern Campeche Bank at the same depths. The Loop Current flows over the sill at a depth of 1400 m into water depths greater than 3000m. The upwelling may be caused by the Loop Current entraining water just below sill depth on the northern side of the sill as the Loop Current moves over deeper water. A generally east-west temperature gradient is observed in the model mean fields from 2500 m through 3100 m. A barotropic, cyclonic current that follows the 3000-m isobath is present in the 12-year mean velocity fields. A conceptual model for the ventilation of the deep water has developed from this study that features downwelling of relatively cold, salty water in the far eastern basin, the deep mean cyclonic current, and upwelling of older, relatively warm water onto the Campeche Bank beneath the western limb of the LC. The dissolved oxygen that is present in the deep water of the GOM is likely derived from the relatively cold, highly oxygenated mixture of UNADW and Caribbean water overflowing the Yucatan sill. This conceptual model is nearly identical to the explanation by Maul et al. (1985) as to why T-S properties at the sill of the Florida Straits and the sill of the Yucatan Channel are different. It would seem at first that there should be a net loss of heat from the deep layer if cold water was added in the far eastern basin and warmer water was being extracted over the northern Campeche Bank. The loss of heat from the deep waters in the eastern basin may be balanced by the transport of heat to the western GOM by LC rings

REFERENCES

Bryan, K. 1969. A numerical model for the study of the world ocean. J. Comput. Phys. 4:347-376.

Berberian, G.A and A.Y. Cantillo. 1999. Oceanographic Conditions in the Gulf of Mexico and Straits of Florida, Fall 1976. NOAA Data Report OAR AOML-36. Atlantic Oceanographic and Meteorological Laboratory, Miami, Fl.

Buerkert, T.P. 1997. Barium in water and foraminiferal shells: indicators of present and past oceanographic conditions in the Gulf of Mexico. Ph.D. Thesis. Louisiana State University. Baton Rouge, La.

Carney, R.S. 1997. Workshop on environmental issues surrounding deepwater oil and gas development: Final report. OCS Study MMS 98-0022. U.S. Dept. of the Interior, Minerals Management Service, Gulf of Mexico OCS Regional Office, New Orleans, La. 163 pp.

Cooper, C., Forristall, G.Z. and T.M. Joyce. 1990. Velocity and hydrographic structure of two Gulf of Mexico ware-core rings. J. Geophys. Res. 95:1663-1679.

Cox, M.D. 1984. A primitive equation three-dimensional model of the ocean. Tech. Rep. 1. Geophys. Fluid Dyn. Lab, NOAA. Princeton, NJ. 250 pp.

Cushman-Roisin, B., E.P. Chassignet, and B. Tang. 1990. Westward motion of mesoscale eddies. J. Phys. Oceanogr. 20:758-768.

Elliot, B. 1982. Anticyclonic rings in the Gulf of Mexico. J. Phys. Oceanogr. 12:1292-1309.

Flierl, G.R. and R.P. Mied. 1985. Frictionally induced circulations and spin down of a warm-core ring. J. Geophys. Res. 90:8,917-8,927.

Hamilton, P. 1990. Deep currents in the Gulf of Mexico. J. Phys. Oceanogr. 20:1087-1104.

Hamilton, P., G.S. Fargion, and D.C. Biggs. 1999. Loop Current eddy paths in the western Gulf of Mexico. J. Phys. Oceanogr. 29:1,180:1,207.

Hamilton, P. and A.Lugo-Fernandez. 2001. Observations of high speed deep currents in the Northern Gulf of Mexico. Geophys. Res. Letters. 28:2,867-2,870.

Hellerman, S. and M. Rosenstein. 1983. Normal monthly wind stress over the world ocean with error estimates. J. Phys. Oceanogr. 13:1,093-1,104.

Hurlburt, H.E. and J.D. Thompson. 1980. A numerical study of Loop Current intrusions and eddy shedding. J. Phys. Oceanogr. 10:1,611-1,651.

Hurlburt, H.E. and J.D. Thompson. 1982. The dynamics of the Loop Current and shed eddies in a numerical model of the Gulf of Mexico, pp. 243-298. In J.C.J. Nihoul, Ed., Hydrodynamics of semi-enclosed seas. Elsevier Scientific Publishing Co. Amsterdam.

Indest, A.W. 1992. Ring dynamics in the western Gulf of Mexico. Ph.D. Thesis. Old Dominion University. Norfolk, Va. 127 pp.

Inoue, M. and S.E. Welsh. 1997. Numerical simulation of Gulf of Mexico circulation under present and glacial climatic conditions. OCS Study MMS 96-0067. U.S. Dept. of the Interior, Minerals Management Service, Gulf of Mexico OCS Region, New Orleans, La. 146 pp.

Inoue, M. and S.E. Welsh, L. Rouse, and E. Weeks. 2002. Observation of deep water manifestation of Loop Current and Loop Current rings in the eastern Gulf of Mexico. EOS, Transactions, American Geophysical Union 52:321.

Kirwan, A.D, J.K. Lewis, AW. Indest, P. Reinersman, and I. Quintero. 1988. Observed and simulated kinematic properties of Loop Current rings. J. Geophys. Res. 93:1,189-1,198.

Lewis, J.K. and A.D. Kirwan. 1987. Genesis of a Gulf of Mexico ring as determined from kinematic analyses. J. Geophys. Res. 92:11,727-11,7240.

Lugo-Fernández, A., M.V. Morin, C.C. Ebesmeyer, and C.F. Marshall. 2001. Gulf of Mexico Historic (1955-1987) Surface Drifter Data Analysis. J. Coastal Res. 17:1-16.

Maul, G.A., D.A. Mayer, and S.R. Baig. 1985. Comparisons between a continuous 3-year current-meter observation at the sill of the Yucatan Strait, satellite measurements of Gulf Loop Current area, and regional sea level. J. Geophys. Res. 90:9,089-9,096.

Nowlin, W.D., A.E. Jochens, S.F. DiMarco, R.O. Reid, and M.K. Howard. 2001. Deepwater physical oceanography reanalysis and synthesis of historical data. OCS Study MMS 2001-064. U.S. Dept. of the Interior, Minerals Management Service, Gulf of Mexico OCS Region, New Orleans, La. 514 pp.

NODC 1994. World Ocean Atlas 1994 CD-ROM Data Sets. NOAA/NESDIS/NODC E/OC21. Washington, D.C.

Oey, L.-Y. 1995. Eddy- and wind-forced shelf circulation. J. Geophys. Res. 100:8,621-8,637.

Oey, L-Y and P. Hamilton. 2000. Modeling and data-analyses of subsurface currents on the northern Gulf of Mexico slope and rise: effects of Topographic Rossby Waves and eddy-slope interaction. Proceedings from the >Workshop on the Physical Oceanography Slope and Rise of the Gulf of Mexico=. September 12-14, 2000. U.S. Dept. of the Interior, Minerals Management Service, Gulf of Mexico OCS Region, New Orleans, La.

Pacanowski, R., K. Dixon, and A. Rosati. 1991. "The GFDL Modular Ocean Model User's Guide version 1.0", GFDL Ocean Group Technical Report #2. Princeton, N.J.

Pacanowski, R. 1996. "MOM 2 Documentation, User's Guide, and Reference Manual, Version 2.0", GFDL Ocean Technical Report #3.2. Princeton, N.J.

Pequegnat, W. E. 1972. A deep bottom current on the Mississippi Cone. Texas A&M Univ. Studies, vol. 2, L. R. A. Capurro and J. L. Reid, Eds., Gulf Publishing Co., Tx. 65-87.

Polzin, K. L., J. M. Toole, J. R. Ledwell, and R. W. Schmitt. 1997. Spatial variability of turbulent mixing in the abyssal ocean. Science. 276:93-96.

Reznik, G.M. and G.G. Sutyrin. 2001. Baroclinic topographic modons. J. Fluid Mech. 437:121-142.

Science Applications International Corporation. 1986. Gulf of Mexico Ship-of-Opportunity Data Report. OCS Report/MMS 86-0028. U.S. Dept. of the Interior, Minerals Mgmt. Service, Gulf of Mexico OCS Regional Office, New Orleans, La. 632 pp.

Schmitz, J.E. and A.C. Vastano. 1976. On entrainment and diffusion in a Gulf of Mexico anticyclonic ring. J. Phys. Oceanogr. 6:399-402.

Schmitz, W.J., J.D. Thompson, and J.R. Luyten. 1992. The Sverdrup circulation for the Atlantic along 24°N. J. Geophys. Res. 97:7251-7256.

Stern, M. E. 1975. Minimal properties of planetary eddies. J. Mar. Res. 33:1-13.

Sturges, W. 1994. The frequency of ring separations from the Loop Current. J. Phys. Oceanogr. 24:1647-1651.

Sturges, W. and R. Leben. 2000. Frequency of ring separations from the Loop Current in the Gulf of Mexico: A revised estimate. J. Phys. Oceanogr. 30:1,814-1,819.

Sturges, W., J.C. Evans, S. Welsh and W. Holland. 1993. Separation of warm-core rings in the Gulf of Mexico. J. Phys. Oceanogr. 23:250-268.

Sutyrin, G. 2001. Effects of topography on the beta-drift of a baroclinic vortex. J. Mar. Res. 59:977-989.

Vidal, V.M.V., F.V. Vidal, A.F. Hernández, E. Meza, and J.J. Pérez-Molero. 1994. Baroclinic flows, transports, and kinematic properties in a cyclonic-anticyclonic-cyclonic ring triad in the Gulf of Mexico. J. Geophys. Res. 99:7,571-7,597.

Vidal, V.M.V., F.V. Vidal, E. Meza, J. Portilla, L. Zambrano, and B. Jaimes. 1999. Ring-slope interactions and the formation of the western boundary current in the Gulf of Mexico. J. Geophys. Res. 99: 7,571-7,597.

Vukovich, F.M. 1995. An Evaluation of the Loop Current=s eddy-shedding frequency. J. Geophys. Res. 100:8,655-8,659.

Vukovich, F.M. and Crissman, B.W. 1986. Aspects of warm rings in the Gulf of Mexico. J. Geophys. Res. 91:2,645-2,660.

Welsh, S.E. 1996. A numerical modeling study of the Gulf of Mexico during present and past environmental conditions. Phd. Thesis. Louisiana State University. Baton Rouge, La. 206 pp.

Welsh, S.E and M. Inoue. 2000. LC rings and the deep circulation in the Gulf of Mexico. J. Geophys. Res. 105:16,951-16,959.

Wust, G. 1964. Stratification and circulation in the Antillean-Caribbean Basins, vol. 1. Columbia University Press, N.Y. 201 pp.

The Department of the Interior Mission

As the Nation's principal conservation agency, the Department of the Interior has responsibility for most of our nationally owned public lands and natural resources. This includes fostering sound use of our land and water resources; protecting our fish, wildlife, and biological diversity; preserving the environmental and cultural values of our national parks and historical places; and providing for the enjoyment of life through outdoor recreation. The Department assesses our energy and mineral resources and works to ensure that their development is in the best interests of all our people by encouraging stewardship and citizen participation in their care. The Department also has a major responsibility for American Indian reservation communities and for people who live in island territories under U.S. administration.

The Minerals Management Service Mission

As a bureau of the Department of the Interior, the Minerals Management Service's (MMS) primary responsibilities are to manage the mineral resources located on the Nation's Outer Continental Shelf (OCS), collect revenue from the Federal OCS and onshore Federal and Indian lands, and distribute those revenues.

Moreover, in working to meet its responsibilities, the **Offshore Minerals Management Program** administers the OCS competitive leasing program and oversees the safe and environmentally sound exploration and production of our Nation's offshore natural gas, oil and other mineral resources. The MMS **Minerals Revenue Management** meets its responsibilities by ensuring the efficient, timely and accurate collection and disbursement of revenue from mineral leasing and production due to Indian tribes and allottees, States and the U.S. Treasury.

The MMS strives to fulfill its responsibilities through the general guiding principles of: (1) being responsive to the public's concerns and interests by maintaining a dialogue with all potentially affected parties and (2) carrying out its programs with an emphasis on working to enhance the quality of life for all Americans by lending MMS assistance and expertise to economic development and environmental protection.